W. R. MITCHELL

It's a long way to MUCKLE FLUGGA

Journeys in Northern Scotland

With a Foreword by
Alfred Wainwright

AMBERLEY

Approaching the Island of Staffa from Mull.

First published 1990
This edition published 2009

Amberley Publishing Plc
Cirencester Road, Chalford,
Stroud, Gloucestershire, GL6 8PE

www.amberley-books.com

Copyright © W. R. Mitchell 2009

The right of W. R. Mitchell to be identified as
the Author of this work has been asserted in
accordance with the Copyrights, Designs and
Patents Act 1988.

ISBN 978 1 84868 455 3

British Library Cataloguing in Publication
Data.

A catalogue record for this book is available
from the British Library.

Typesetting and Origination by FonthillMedia.
Printed in the UK.

To
Helen, Kathryn and Gillian

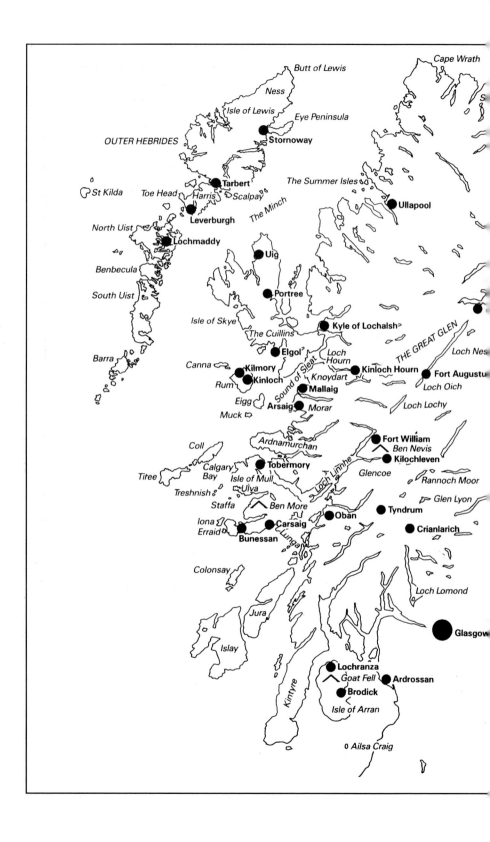

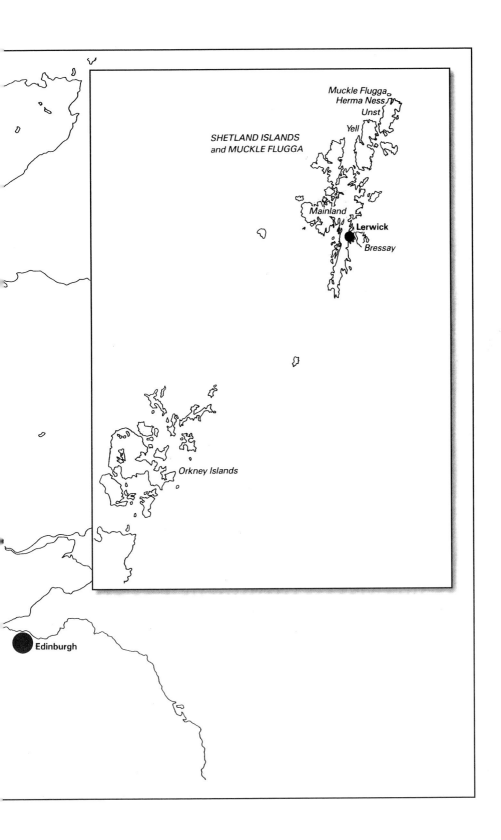

SHETLAND ISLANDS
and MUCKLE FLUGGA

Muckle Flugga
Herma Ness
Unst
Yell

Mainland

Lerwick
Bressay

Orkney Islands

Edinburgh

Buchaille Etive Mor.

A red stag with its antlers partly grown – said to be 'in velvet'.

Gannet at its nest.

Puffin on the Treshnish Islands.

Storm beach, the Summer Isles.

'... it is no wonder that the Highlands have been called melancholy,
But two fellows have wandered through them, laughed at every
opportunity, rhymed and sketched together, growled at one another
and at the world if they happened to be vexed or found nothing to
eat, devoured everything in sight when they did find it and slept 12
hours every night, These two were we—
And we'll not forget it as long as we live...'

Felix Mendelssohn, 1829

CONTENTS

FOREWORD

by A. Wainwright

Bill Mitchell has been a journalist of consistent excellence throughout his working life, with an outstanding talent for research and description that established him as a leading literary figure in the north of England. When he became Editor of two popular monthly magazines, Dalesman and Cumbria, he continued to contribute articles and books on the life and landscapes of the Yorkshire Dales and the Lake District with an occasional foray over the Border.

He has long had a love affair with the remote places of the Highlands and Islands of Scotland, travelling not as a tourist but as a nomadic wanderer inspired by a special interest in the ornithology and the fauna and flora of these lonely regions.

In this present volume he recalls many of his adventures and explorations and discoveries that remain fresh in his memory and tells of them in an entertaining and often amusing style. Manifest through the pages is his consuming interest in the natural life and scenery of the crafting communities and wilderness areas of the western seaboard and its mountainous hinterland.

This is an enjoyable account of his travels, and will appeal not only to those who have an affinity with the places he describes so well but also to others who like to sit in an armchair with a jolly good book.

Quiraing, Isle of Skye.

INTRODUCTION

Fred spread his arms and said: 'I know just what a wild goose feels like when it's getting ready to fly northwards in spring.' He and his brother Ron had collected me, as usual, for our springtime jaunt in the Highlands. We met for one short period of the year and at other times made no special attempt to contact each other, not even exchanging Christmas cards.

A few days beforehand, Fred would ring me up to assure himself I was still alive. He would then say: 'Pick you up at 8.20 on Good Friday'—and we were on our way. The destination changed from year to year—we ranged far and wide across western Scotland and the Isles—but none of us concerned ourselves with such matters, for at Perth (pronounced Payrrth) lives George, a braw Scot with a fierce love of his native land.

George had the imaginative ideas and he made the arrangements, whether it was hiring a 'wee bothy', complete with black cat, by Loch Hourn, or a newish bungalow on the machair of western Harris. To George, it was 'nae bother'. Sometimes it was 'nae problem'. It was George who added the essential ingredient, Scottishness, to our excursions. Through him, we met local people; we became familiar with the interiors of Heiland inns and (except for teetotal me) with the warming sensation of whisky in the throat.

To me, drinking whisky was as pleasant an experience as imbibing paraffin would be, and if I accepted a 'wee drammie' to be sociable, I contrived to tip it over the nearest pot plant. I sometimes hanker to return and note the effect on the plants. Did they die with the botanical equivalent of a burp? Or is there a strain of super-plants north of the Border?

In one far-western home—a house with the sea on three sides—George introduced me to a couple who soon revealed their detestation of Whitehall Rule. The normal civility and hospitality were absent. So I began to tell of how my native Yorkshire had suffered from Southerners—of William the Conqueror's Harrying of the North and how the Pilgrimage of Grace was ruthlessly put down, its leaders hanged. I warmed to the topic, told of the upper dales where farmsteads were roofless, walls gapped and the moor was claiming its own again....

The wife listened intently and then said: 'Och! Have a wee dram!'

Each spring, for a week or two, we reverted to the wild, glorying in a landscape that was waking up after the long northern winter, laughing our way from glen to glen, cracking jokes about wild haggis and waging war against sheep-ticks. We stood at the rims of lonely mountains and let our eyes range over half of Scotland.

We had this vague notion of reaching Muckle Flugga, the most northerly point in Britain—excluding a mere lump of wave-smoothed rock which is prosaically known as the Outstack. Muckle Flugga, a short ridge protruding for 200 feet from a cruel sea, is distinguished by a lighthouse. My first view of the Flugga was in a television film, a bird's eye view of Britain, devised and narrated by John Betjeman. He, the BBC and an indomitable helicopter pilot, eventually reached Herma Ness, on the island of Unst. They then flew low, over a bird-speckled sea, to Flugga and Outstack, names that have a chilly Norse air about them. Long after the credits had rolled at the end of the film, long after the last crashing note of music had faded, I sat thinking of the Flugga. It was the name that appealed: I thrilled to its far-northern situation off the remote north-west of Europe.

Ron speculated on the first visitors to the Scottish islands, long before Mr MacBrayne came along to give some distinction to inter-island travel. Fred mused on the type of craft—a dug-out canoe, with space for grannie at the back. We know something about the few family groups who reached the north-western seaboard of Europe—Britain was not then an island—because we have sifted through their rubbish dumps. They were desperately short of protein; their dreams would be coloured by thoughts of slaying a red deer, and securing 300 pounds of good red meat. That was the culinary jackpot. Frail humans had usually to be content with collecting shellfish along the shore. Someone worked out that 140 limpets must be eaten to provide the food value of a single pound of lean meat!

The eighteenth century was a time of widespread excitement about travel and discovery. Bookshops were clogged with tomes about exotic parts of the world, written by those who had explored them. It was only human to tell a good story and, at times, to invent a little to breathe novelty into a wilting passage.

The first tourists in the Highlands and Islands were following a tradition that had sent travellers to the extremities of Britain—and especially the mountainous areas, like Wales, the Pennines and Lake District of England. Men of 'taste and curiosity', who might have gone on the Grand Tour, were unable to do so because of war with France; they were alerted by pioneer guide book writers like Thomas Pennant to the attractions that lay at home, for the enjoyment of which one had to undertake journeys no less arduous than those on the Continent. They benefited from improved roads, especially those made to the instructions of General Wade in the wake of the Jacobite troubles.

Towards the end of the century, mere travel was not enough. The Picturesque Movement developed. It was just that—the appreciation of landscape as a series of pictures from set vantage points. Sometimes, with a Claude glass, a traveller actually turned his or her back on the view and studied its reflection!

Scotland had an appeal because travellers found themselves among a people who were theoretically British but spoke a strange tongue! James Boswell, chronicler of the Highland travels of Dr Johnson, reported thus about a visit to Auchnasheal: 'We had a considerable circle about us, men women and children, all McCraes, Lord Seaforth's people. I observed to Dr Johnson, it was much the same as being with a tribe of Indians. —Johnson. "Yes, sir: but not so terrifying."'

Thomas Pennant actually bought 'ribbons and other trifles' to give to the natives. 'I lamented that my money had been so uselessly laid out; for a few dozens of fishhooks or a few pecks of meal would have made them happy.' The tourist discovery of Scotland's north-western seaboard might be said to date from Pennant's visits. In 1769, he noted that this was 'a country... as little known to its southern brethren as Kamtschatka.' It was written of Pennant that he 'published an account of his journey which proved that the northern part of Great Britain might be visited with safety, and even with pleasure.'

Pennant gloried in his good health; he was temperate in his ways and did not drink; he went to bed at 10 p.m. and rose, winter and summer alike, at 7 a.m. He avoided eating supper, 'the meal of excess'. He also took the weight off his feet by riding a horse.

On our travels, Fred quietly insisted that we dine at hotels rather than consuming plastic food from plastic plates at some of the lesser hostelries. Boswell and Johnson, fond of good food and liquor, found both at the homes of the well-to-do following introductions by friends.

At the house of Mackinnon of Coirechatachan, 'we had for supper a large dish of minced beef collops, a large dish of fricassee of fowl, I believe a dish called fried chicken or something like it, a dish of ham or tongue, some excellent haddocks, some herrings, a large bowl of rich milk, frothed, as good a bread-pudding as I ever tasted, full of raisins and lemons or orange peel, and sillabubs made with port wine and in sillabub glasses. There was a good table-cloth with napkins; china, silver spoons, porter if we chose it, and a large bowl of very good punch.' More culinary delights were available at Raasay House, which they reached several days later...

The two visitors were somewhat amused by the Highland custom of having a 'wee dram' at the slightest provocation. 'A man of the Hebrides... as soon as he appears in the morning, swallows a glass of whisky; yet they are not a drunken race, at least I never was present at much intemperance,' wrote the good doctor. 'But no man is so abstemious as to refuse the morning dram, which they call a skalk.'

He explained that the word whisky signifies water, and is applied by way of eminence to 'strong water' or distilled liquor. 'The spirit drunk in the North is drawn from barley. I never tasted it, except once for experiment at the inn in Inverary, when I thought it preferable to the English malt brandy... What was the process I had no opportunity of inquiring, nor do I wish to improve the art of making poison pleasant.'

I envy Johnson and Boswell the novelty of being in areas where tourism was as yet unknown. Boswell, writing in 1773, had heard there was nothing worthy of observation on Ulva, off the west of Mull, so they took boat and voyaged the short distance to Inchkenneth. 'As we walked up from the shore, Dr Johnson's heart was cheered by the sight of a road marked with cart wheels, as on the main land; a thing which we had not seen for a long time. It gave us a pleasure similar to that which a traveller feels whilst, wandering on what he fears is a desert island, he perceives the print of human feet.'

The early tourists carried with them a copy of Pennant's 'Tour' and tended to follow slavishly what soon became a well-worn tourist route. A highlight of any Hebridean tour was a visit to Staffa and Fingal's Cave. Dr Thomas Garnett (1798) was among those who sailed to the island; the cave 'appears like the inside of a cathedral of immense size, but superior to any work of art in grandeur and sublimity and equal to any in regularity.'

Today, we are inclined to take travel for granted and do not approach natural features with as great a sense of wonder as did the pioneers on the tourist trails.

My earliest adventuring on the Scottish islands had been second-hand, through the pages of books written by Richard Kearton who, with his brother Cherry, was among the first great popularisers of natural history. As a small boy, with a vivid imagination, I was able to accompany these astonishing Yorkshiremen to the rocky fringes of northern Britain. In later years, corresponding with members of the family, I could create a more rounded picture. For a while, it was enough to have the words and the pictures in books borrowed from the library.

Richard suffered a serious injury to a leg through a fall during a boyhood nesting jaunt in his native Swaledale. It was left to Cherry to perform any necessary athletic feats, such as inspecting cliff faces from the end of a hempen rope. After the heady days of seeking out birds and beasts in remote Britain, Cherry went off to Africa and made a name for himself as writer and photographer. Richard remained faithful to his native land.

His first visit to Unst, most northerly island of the Shetland group, had been in 1898. Fifteen years later he was back with his daughter, heading for Herma Ness to photograph the great skuas. There had been 13 or 14 pairs, cared for by 'Henry the watcher', and in 1913 the number had risen to more than 70 pairs, with Henry still in attendance to discourage visitors from interfering with the nests.

Richard described the great skua, or 'bonxie', as 'a kind of buccaneer', and went into detail about its way of securing food—by harrying other birds and causing them to disgorge whatever they had in their crop, whereupon the skua had a ready-made warm meal! Richard told of the skua's power dive on intruders. 'The act of stooping near the nest as if examining a chick is always sure to arouse the anger of the parent birds and bring them down like a whirlwind to attack the naturalist.' A bonxie might knock off one's headgear from behind or from right or left, 'but so far as my experience carries me it never makes a frontal attack.'

He encountered the Arctic or Richardson's skua and, knowing that readers like a touch of novelty, recorded of the birds at Herma Ness: 'I do not know what the reader will think of my veracity when I solemnly state that it is possible to induce such a wild robber of the air to give up its lawless depredation for a time and virtuously subsist upon a diet of Scotch scone charitably supplied by human hands.'

He was referring to old Henry's custom, over the years, of sharing his snack meals with a pair of Arctic skuas nesting near the little hut he occupied during the nesting season. Kearton and his daughter kept up the custom, and then tried to tempt the Arctic skuas with variations on the bannock theme. The birds refused bread and butter 'and when I smeared marmalade upon it they despised it.'

The Keartons had their share of bad weather, midges and the frustration of not having any film left to record some unexpected happening.

On our return journey from Mid Yell to Lerwick, the captain of the steamer told me he thought he would be able to show us some seals on an isolated rock lying in our course. The water being deep, he very obligingly took the boat close in, slowed down and blew the siren. There were from 12 to 15 adult seals on the rock. One or two plunged headlong into the sea and swam away, but the majority boldly remained behind and stared at us with evident curiosity. Alas! we had not a single unexposed plate or an inch of kinematograph film left.

I now wince at some of the tactics used by the naturalist to secure good photographs. Kearton took a movie camera to the Outer Hebrides and attempted to take a sequence of pictures of a pair of black-throated divers and their young as they swam on a loch. A hide was erected, and the keepers in a boat drove the birds towards the hide. To Kearton's disappointment, the birds dived when near the hide.

One of the Highlanders suggested they might tire a young diver by pursuing it up and down the loch for an hour. Kearton, astonishingly agreed to this, but 'long before the young bird was exhausted its parents swam round a little promontory, behind which they were hidden from our sight for a few minutes". They hid the youngster somewhere on the rough coastline, and we recognised in sadness that we were defeated.'

At times our spirits were low—I particularly recall eating tomato sandwiches in driving rain on Bloodstone Hill, Rum—but another time, in Sutherland, we were so elated we forgot even to open our packed meals. We had been making for Sandwood Bay, and our long walk over dreary moorland ended on white sand beside a blue sea, with a cloudless sky above.

One day, on Wettest Rum, Fred and I walked into a situation of which dreams are made. We covered six miles in wind and rain, had our boots topped up with water while crossing a swollen burn, and eventually entered a remote bothy just as two attractive lasses were heating up soup which they shared with us. When the mist was down, we sometimes walked much farther than we had intended.

George described any sort of lodging as a bothy. (He also used the term about his own splendid home!) When we catered for ourselves, and took possession of some modest dwelling—a wee cottage or a shepherd's hut—we would set about airing the place as a matter of urgency. Windows were opened, a fire was soon roaring in the hearth, the boiler hissed and bubbled, and any loose pipes clanged.

One lodging had an electricity meter that took 50p coins almost as fast as we could feed them in, yet—infuriatingly—the airing cupboard was sealed off. Another bothy had a calendar on the wall indicating that it had last been consulted the previous autumn. Now it was spring: we were the first visitors of the year. We were especially keen to take the dampness from the corners of those rooms.

It pleased Ron to read of the adventures of eighteenth-century tourists, who invariably commented on the damp beds. Boswell, touring the Hebrides with Dr Johnson, and staying with Dr Maclean, was shocked by the dirtiness of the bed linen. 'I threw off only my boots and coat and waistcoat and put on my greatcoat as a night-gown, and so lay down. The mixture of brandy punch at the inn and rum punch here, joined with the comfortless bed, made me rest very poorly.'

James Hogg, the self-educated 'Ettrick Shepherd', at Stornoway in mid-June, could not sleep because a 'desperate affray' involving several respectable local men was taking place in the next room. 'Desperate wounds were given and received, the door was split in pieces and twice some of the party entered my chamber.'

The number of adventurers on our springtime jaunt varied from year to year, through family or business commitments, but Fred and I managed to attend them all. It was through

George's imaginative excursions to the rocky rim of Scotland that I had afternoon tea on the island of Canna with an amiable old lady called Mary Anne, and stood in the hall of an Edwardian castle on the Isle of Rum at midnight, while George arranged for Wagner to be performed on an electric organ. He introduced me to Lea McNally at Torridon, to the Minister on Eigg and to a bagpipe-playing hotelier at Glenfinnan.

He was at the tiller of the small boat that passed by starlight through a tidal rip known as the Jaws of Hell. He arranged for us to visit the Falls of Glomach, which roar out like prophets in a wilderness of gorges and soaring peaks. One evening, we attended the big hoose for a meal that took place under the gaze of an indomitable woman and portraits of her Jacobean ancestors. She greeted us dressed in a long gown, which seemed needlessly formal. I soon realised that she had dressed not for dinner but for draughts! My legs became numb with cold. It was a remarkable place: a house half full of cats between a loch half full of sea trout and a hill half full of red deer—plus the odd eagle.

I should also introduce John, our companion on several jaunts, who alas fell victim to coronary trouble but who lived on in our memories and field notes. It was John who, feeling off colour, knocked at a Highland surgery door and came face to face with a doctor who did not invite him to cross the step. The doctor listened to John's spluttering self-diagnosis and then rasped: 'What you want is f-r-e-s-h air!

George, who has long regarded the Highlands as an extension of his back garden on Kinnoull Hill, was to show us a considerable wealth of wildlife. We motored from Yorkshire to Perth, where a night's lodging was booked. It was the time of year when the grey geese were restive, anxious to return to their breeding haunts in Iceland. There might be several hundred in the field near George's well-elevated house.

Later, with George as our guide, we would see red deer grazing in snow-rimmed corries; we watched the ballet of Manx shearwaters off the Small Isles; we saw the white hares of Perthshire feeding in the gloaming. It was George who pointed out the golden eagle gliding across a tousled hillside and almost stroking the heather; the big bird was gliding—into the wind! As we had our first stop for food in the lee of some rocks at the summit of a hill that loomed high above Loch Hourn, we heard the gabbling of geese. A score of birds passed over us within sandwich-tossing range.

We travelled ever northwards, thinking all the time of Fred's migrating goose. We responded joyfully to an absence of crowds. 'There's a tourist,' said Fred, who had been visiting the Highlands and Islands long enough to regard himself as an honorary native. We would sit in quiet contemplation of the landscape or a sea loch, thrilled by the quality of space and light. There were compensations for those gentle Celtic monks who witnessed to their faith in remote places. They could daily lift up their eyes to the hills; they were at one with nature, finding kinship with bird and beast, as their nature poems testify.

The 300 years of witness by the Celtic Church had ended when the Norsemen arrived. In Shetland, looking from the fulmar-haunted cliffs above Northwick, we pondered on the arrival of the Scandinavians in their longships with dragonesque prows and striped sails; they were only a day's sail from Norway, and were out of sight of land for only about a third of the way. Even then, the seabirds, hurrying back to their nesting cliffs with sea-food, would take them unerringly to the nearest shore.

Fred preferred the bellow of the Norse horn to the skirl of the bagpipes: it was the only aspect of Scottish life that made him wince. His definition of a Scottish gentleman was 'a person who knows how to play the pipes—but doesn't!'

Comedians make the most of the Scottish fondness for whisky, but it is undoubtedly the 'curse o' the islands'. Most of the drinkers appeared to be able to imbibe considerable quantities without distress. To enter a home as a friend or guest was sufficient reason for the head of the house to reach for bottle and glasses. 'Och, have a wee dram...'

George, who never drinks to excess, nonetheless told me of true Highland hospitality, when 'you open a bottle of whisky—and throw the cork on the fire!' When George wanted to show his appreciation to an islander who, using his powerful tractor, had just hauled the visitor's car from a marshy spot, he invited him in for a dram. On the way, the man's brother mysteriously appeared. Perhaps he could lip-read from a range of one and a-half miles! The two men sat sipping their wee drammies, while the afternoon slowly passed and the engine of the unattended tractor ticked over, the exhaust pipe breathing blue smoke into the otherwise clear Hebridean air. George surreptitiously slipped the tractor driver £15 'for your trouble'. The driver was so delighted, he accepted another drammie and muttered, 'Fifteen pounds! That's £10 for me and £5 for him!'

It is not unusual for an Islander to go on the spree and to re-emerge from wherever he had hidden himself looking as though he had come face to face with death. I once walked a mile-and-a-half to a local shop, hoping to buy some cigarettes, but found the shop closed. There was no sign of life until some shrubbery rustled and the brother of the shop-owner appeared, grey and with a considerable stubble of hair on his chin. He had been drinking steadily outdoors for several days. Now he had red-rimmed eyes and a tongue so dry it was like sandpaper. We shared our common distress—both of us were without cigarettes—and then we parted. His last words were: 'I've chust been having a wee drink...'

I watched a fisherman drink a bottle of whisky without flinching and marvelled at the robust quality of his digestive system. The spirits went into his body like water down a drain. I saw men queuing at a roadside inn for 'morning surgery', dispensed from the bottle. To see an alcoholic wife indulging her craving for drink while the husband sat silently nearby and the children played on the floor of the bar and rubbed their eyes through fatigue because of the lateness of the hour, was to feel a surge of pity for the whole family. And to resolve never to tell another funny story about whisky.

The drinking habits of a whole populace were evident from the roadside litter—the cans of beer and the bottles that had contained the hard stuff—whisky bottles with labels showing symbols of the Scottish heritage, used unfeelingly by the sales departments. I was told the story of the Scottish whisky-drinker who died and was cremated. 'Och, but it took 'em three days to put the fire out...' The old man who was speaking suddenly wheezed like an old thorn tree being strummed by the wind. He was laughing.

I stared with disbelief as we took possession of one bothy with provisions that included 21 bottles of whisky, made freely available to all comers. Visitors were numerous as the word spread. George frequently appeared at the bothy with friends who had been strangers five minutes before. They arrived protestingly—'Och, but...' They stayed and had wee drammies. The whisky supply was exhausted by mid-week.

We—the lads and myself—pondered on what we termed 'the island sickness'. It was in part a consequence of a community run down and demoralised by changing social conditions. The young folk had been shipped off to school on the mainland and had now left home; there remained an ageing populace, living on State hand-outs or some offspins of the tourist trade. All too often the tourist possibilities were being exploited by in-comers.

When the ownership of an island changed, there could be unhappy consequences in a community which for many years had known the previous family well. And there was the discomfort of a long, dark, frosty northern winter to bear. It was all right in the old days, when people came together to enjoy themselves with dancing, singing, food and drink. 'Now there are so few people about; there's chust the telly...'

It is so easy to find blissful relief from present problems in a whisky-induced stupor...

We had our own rituals, chief of which was the Bread Hurling Competition. It all started one day when we ate the sandwich fillings and disgustedly threw the sticky, steam-baked bread to the gulls. As we were on a cliff edge, we watched, entranced, as the airborne bread travelled a considerable distance. Henceforth, bread-hurling became competitive, though it was decreed that none of it should be toasted, since this gave a decided advantage!

In the accounts that follow, take the preliminaries for granted. Each year, we would dash up the road to Perth to receive a welcome from George and his wife Maisie, and an evening meal featuring special Scottish fare. The next morning, refreshed and aglow with anticipation, we would set forth.

1 RED DEER IN THE SUNSET
The Isle of Arran

The big boat, outward bound from Ardrossan, ironed out a spirited sea. We sailed into a north-west wind, with gannets from Ailsa Craig gliding over the white-topped waves. They had no need to beat their wings; they progressed on an uprush of air, showing off their Omo-white plumage, with the straw-yellow heads and black wing-tips. A bird dived, a jet of water marking its point of entry.

Only a species-hungry ornithologist was on the open deck. No one seemed in the mood for food. Fred and I had already dined: we had been to an Indian Restaurant (where everyone spoke with a Scottish accent) and had an old Indian dish (mushroom omelette with chips). As we ate, the ferryboat *Isle of Arran* was fidgeting at her moorings, with the bow section raised, admitting traffic. It looked as though the boat was yawning.

By the time we reached Brodick Pier, we had lapsed—between ourselves—into pidgin Scots, of the Music Hall variety. Our hotel, a large building with a somewhat faded grandeur, overlooked the bay. A few eider drakes, one duck and one duckling, bobbed like corks on the short, sharp waves. The duckling needed great bursts of energy to keep pace with its mother and avoid being eaten by a swooping gull, a fate which appeared to have befallen its brothers and sisters.

At a time of year when few holidaymakers were astir,

someone had dreamed up a fortnight's golfing festival. Every ferryboat had a contingent of golfers. To walk along the front without a trolley was to invite comment.

We had come to an island which, according to every book and brochure, is a microcosm of Scotland. In the north is a rockscape, dominated by Goat Fell, the Highland flavour completed by eagles and red deer. Southwards, the landscape softens and is flatter, being not unlike Ireland, the northern coastline of which can be seen across the water. Arran's settlements are by the sea; the hinterland is sparse on buildings and people, although stone circles testify to the life that was, some 4,000 years ago.

To describe Arran as a microcosm of Scotland is to think in the most general terms of Highland and Lowland. This large island has the flavour of the Hebrides, especially in the west. We wandered between the Cock of Arran and Bennan Head, the most northerly and southerly points, a mere 19 miles apart to a straight-necked crow. One of the surprises was a walk to Glenashdale Falls, in the south. We looked for signs of Irishness in the landscape and found instead a braw Scottish flavour where water that had flowed through an untamed tract of land took a great leap into a well-wooded valley.

We followed the northern road and found ourselves in the company of jagged peaks that looked purple in the dull light. A few were cocooned by mist. Red stags grazed on quiet hillsides; all but the youngest beasts had cast their antlers. The youngsters retained their simple, unbranched horns.

Eiders were common at the sea's edge. The drakes maintained station like two-tone buoys, and the dowdy ducks had new-hatched young in train—up to a dozen bundles of life covered in black down.

Early next morning, it was the turn of the herring gulls. They proclaimed the new day with a high-pitched wailing or by uttering a laughing call, as though they had just heard a doubtful joke. Noticing that Goat Fell had a bonnet of cloud and was not yet in the right mood to be climbed, we headed in the opposite direction and, in a 14-mile walk, visited Bennan Head.

The air had such clarity, I had a fanciful notion that I could have tossed my cap over the lighthouse on Pladda Island—or even on to Ailsa Crag, the plug of an old volcano, known widely as Paddy's Milestone after the many Irish folk who have sailed past it when emigrating to Glasgow.

Fred looked at the rock beach towards Bennan Head and dubbed it Plastic Beach because of the range of plastic objects, from dustbin-liners to milk bottle carriers, tossed up by the fretful sea. On our way, we passed rocks that were patterned by orange lichen. Sea pinks were coming into bloom and on marshy ground were short spears of green—emergent flag iris—which brightens up many a Highland coastal view in spring. Shelduck left their huge footprints on the wet sands, and a frog-like croaking drew our attention to the fulmars on the high cliffs.

We entered a zone of big boulders, each up to quarter-bungalow size, with limpets looking like warts and lichen the colour of iodine. A cave was the resort of jackdaws, and nearby, a stream poured over a section of cliff darkened by moisture and the growth of plant life. The water seethed as it sprayed the beach, keeping an area permanently damp and rich in flowers—mainly bluebells and pink campions.

We followed the tracks of beef cattle through a jungle of blackberry canes, the trailing stems repeatedly tugging at our boot-laces. We encountered a school party. The teacher said: 'Have you seen any other schoolchildren?' We shook our heads. 'No? Well—you're lucky. They're even noisier than this lot!'

A snack meal and a short nap provided an interlude before we went on through a stretch of squelchy flag iris and prickly gorse, into an area where blackthorn stood in a gown of frothy-white bloom. Fred reported a strange slapping sound. We traced it to a sheep which had a plastic container around one of its hoofs.

Ahead lay a broad beach of golden sand where the 'kleep' of oystercatchers from the tide's edge was persistent. Then we left the beach for a track leading to the road. Our final stretch was through a lush countryside, with well-manicured hedges of beech and thorn. As we descended to Kildonan, we overtook a grandmother, who had collected a small girl from school. She pointed out two adjacent small islands, collectively known as Spoon Island from their distinctive shape when viewed from this angle.

Fred had a hankering to see a good sunset, for at Brodick, on the east coast, we had a premature dusk. When our gulls were getting sleep mist in their eyes, the gulls of Mackrie and Catacol were doubtless still having their suppers, bathed in a romantic afterglow. We motored to Mackrie and noticed that although a mass of static cloud was tethered to Kintyre, the sky beneath was clear and would soon receive the orange-red orb of the sun.

At first, the main hue was lemon, which coloured the sea; then, as the sun dipped, the landscape turned to gold. We decided to keep the sun in view for a little longer by motoring on to Lochranza. In this way, and because of the undulations on Kintyre, we contrived to have four or five sundowns, each richer than the last.

At Lochranza, where the ruins of a castle give distinction to what is now a small holiday centre, the hills were glowing with an unreal red tint from the almost-expired sun, Yet the sky above was an icy blue. The sunset glow was reflected from the hills into the water; the loch was red! We turned to find the dark clouds to the west liberally streaked, as though they were bleeding, and a band of red lay over the clear purple hills of Kintyre. The open sea appeared to be aflame.

We 'glassed' the hills and saw truly red stags—red red deer, in fact. The whole world was populated by strange red creatures—red people, red sheep, red gulls. We contrived to be in the right position as the sun bathed the castle and sea in its blood-red rays.

On our homeward way, in the gloaming, we crossed a moorland road with stags feeding no more than ten yards from the car. Tatty beasts they were, with the winter hair coming away in tufts. Not until the height of summer would they deserve the title of red deer, for then there would be a rufous tinge to their coats. Fred has a theory that they were called red deer because of the blood-sucking activities of the multitudinous ticks.

There was quite a to-do during the night, with chatter and laughter from late-returning golfing revellers. Fred, tolerant as ever, called it a typical Scottish Friday night. I was less accommodating. When the boat came in at 8 a.m., it disgorged more golfers with trolleys, and ramblers looking like snails from the quantity of kit on their backs.

Just north of the Bay stands Brodick Castle, the ancient seat of the Dukes of Hamilton and now the property of the National Trust for Scotland. Some rough old building stood on the site in Viking times. A fourteenth-century stronghold became more of a home from the seventeenth century onwards, and by the nineteenth it was like many another stately Scottish home—tall, substantial but at the same time elegant with its romantic embellishments.

Rising beyond Brodick Castle is Goat Fell, a name which means 'windy hill'. On a day when it was so calm that even cigarette smoke hung about in the great outdoors, Fred and I decided to climb to the attic of Arran—an honest climb, 874 metres (2,866 feet)—from sea level!

We were the first visitors of the day and contrived to become 'lost', so that we might maintain a Yorkshire tradition and have a free look at the castle gardens, and especially the massed rhododendrons and azaleas, now in full bloom. (Later, we discovered that the gardens can be visited free of charge anyway!) A black dog appeared followed by a willowy young woman who directed us with charm and courtesy to the Goat Fell track—and then screamed abuse at the dog when it did not respond immediately to her command. The big black dog cringed; it was a softie at heart.'

Our route to the summit lay through rhododendron grove, spruce plantation, birch belt, heather zone, expanses of coarse grass and steep slopes strewn with boulders. A passing school party included a young lass who advised a lad, as the going became steep, to 'keep yer 'eeard doon, Dougie.' The youngsters were the first to reach the top, of course. Here they commenced to incinerate cigarettes by the yard.

When they had rested, cast their cigarette-ends to the winds and gone clattering down the ankle-ricking slope we had the mountaintop to ourselves. It was warm and windless; there was pleasure in having a snooze with the warm rocks as a couch. Two ravens called as they let the wind carry them across the craggy landscape. One bird flipped on its back for no reason I could deduce except high spirits.

It took us two hours to descend, by a route as knobbly as a burn-bed. During the descent, our toes were forced against the front of our boots and soon we were hobbling.

We reached the coastal road with some relief: at least it was smooth. We strode in hot sunshine, beside a turquoise sea which rippled only when a bird decided to go for a paddle. We beheld the yellow of iris and gorse; we heard the ringing voices of the waders—the sandpipers and oystercatchers.

The eggs of the oystercatchers were hard-set and the incubating birds disinclined to leave. We were able to find at least two nests every mile and one bird was quite aggressive. Its nest was close to the road, which hereabouts was about a yard higher than the beach. Consequently, we were only a few feet away when our eyes met the red-rimmed eyes of the brooding oystercatcher. To say it was annoyed would be a considerable understatement.

The bird stood and uttered a shrill 'Kleep!' Its mandibles, as red as sealing wax, seemed to vibrate as it gave a lusty round of calling, and then it went through the 'broken wing' routine, anxious to divert attention from the nest to itself. I peered over the edge of the road at the clutch of eggs. The oystercatcher came running down the road and then flew at me, hovering a few yards above my head, wings fluttering, pink legs trailing, beak ajar as it gave yet another round of shouting. I had never seen such behaviour before.

Fred and I strode around the Bay, Goat Fell remaining in full view on this strangely warm, cloudless and windless afternoon.

It was early May. Spring had rushed up the glens but was even yet fighting for the high ground. As we climbed an old pony route at the northern end of Arran, we noticed that the birks were greening. A cuckoo called in that soft voice which, nonetheless, has considerable carrying power. Red deer interrupted their grazing and looked at us with eyes that seemed as ancient as the rocks about them. Among the birds in flight were raven and hooded crow—the swashbuckling 'whoodie', which is like a crow wearing a grey jumper.

We made a bee-line for the shore—if bees are in the habit of slithering down a steep peaty slope, between parties of astonished red deer, with dead bracken fronds crackling underfoot. The big stags had cast, but we had neither the time nor the inclination to look for the antlers. Down we slithered, between ancient birch trees that provided song perches for willow warblers and chaffinches. Fred slipped on his back. He did not injure himself but commented that he had re-modelled the sandwiches. He was carrying them in his haversack.

We had our first snack on the seaside rocks, with Fred teasing the eider drakes by giving an imitation of their crooning voice: 'Ah-oo-ah.' He said it was the sound made by a duchess who had just had her bottom pinched! Fred crooned—and two drakes became vocal. At each crooning, a bird drew back its head and simultaneously raised itself in the water.

We marvelled at the Old Red Sandstone that had been polished by numberless tides. Our table was a flat rock some 400 million years old. Rock pipits called around us, their lively ditties clearly audible above the sea's roaring. Ringed plover gave soft purring calls in an area of the shore where, undoubtedly, they had nests. Anyone who watches a ringed plover settle on its eggs must entertain the thought that this diminutive bird is not quite large enough for the task!

A dark, shiny head, showing near the beach, marked where a common seal was watching our progress towards Lochranza. The main colony of seals was sunbathing on a stretch of shore exposed at low tide, lying in an assortment of postures on seaweed and pebbles. Fred and I counted 16 with at least three males, identifiable by their size and bulk. The largest was a silver-grey beast with dark specks on its back and an almost white head.

In due course we came within no more than 25 yards of the nearest group, which included a seal that was balanced on a ridiculously small stone, so that its head and tail were inclined upwards. I watched a seal that was lying on its side, apparently fast asleep but languidly scratching its underside with a flipper.

On our return to the car, we passed a house called 'Geol-na-Mara'. The owner told us the name means 'Music of the Sea'. Then we saw a house called 'Alt-na-Mara', and we discovered this means 'Burn by the Sea'. An old man was feeding two herring gulls with potato crisps. He said that when he had suffered from influenza, and been unable to go out for a day or two, one of the birds had rapped its beak on the living room window.

We passed a lime tree from which came the contented droning of thousands of bees collecting nectar from the blossom. A passing islander said that lime is known locally as the Singing Tree.

Voices were raised at Lochranza in 1307 when Robert the Bruce arrived from Rathlin Island, off the north Irish coast, at the renewal of his campaign for Scottish independence. Bruce is associated with two castles and a cave. Fred and I had to contend with a strong but dry wind on our walk to the coast when we decided to look for the King's Cave—the very place, according to tradition, where he had been impressed by the industry of a spider. (With dozens of caves to choose from, we may have inspected the wrong place. And we did not find a species of spider that can cope with salt spray.)

We took yet another oystercatcher by surprise and found its nest, containing three eggs. Gannets were fishing in the lee of Arran; we saw them making shallow dives, with wings partly folded, to be brought smartly to their sides when the water was reached. The birds' entry to the sea was attended by jets of spray. Fulmars glided effortlessly on wings that were extended stiffly, as though they were made of balsa wood. Water dripped into caves fashioned by nature from the Red Sandstone and colonised by mosses and ferns.

We were entertained by an amorous Hereford bull, which was demolishing a grassy bank by rubbing its head and making circumscribed movements of its forelegs. The bull roared and Fred said it must have caught a whiff of his after-shave. (There was a rival bull in the next field.)

We walked into the middle of a blasted heath, facing a 'lazy' wind—one that cuts through you rather than taking the trouble to go round; the straw put out for the stock was being rolled across the treeless ground like tumbleweed in the desert. Where the foundations of a stone circle were being exposed by archaeologists, we saw flints that had come to light through careful probing with trowels. Dare we ask why the foundations were being exposed when they had been protected for so long by a mass of peat? Archaeologists are good at parrying questions. We asked a young lady about the ultra-tidy appearance of the stone circle. She smiled sweetly and said: 'We cleared away the peat because there would be no peat here when the stone circle was built.'

In the lounge, on our last evening, we discovered Mr Downie's book, *All About Arran*, published in 1933. He had had the Englishman's difficulty in pronouncing Gaelic names and gave a few examples, such as Keer Vawr for Cir Mhor, Ca-is-tel Avel for Caisteal Abhail and Swi-e Fergus for Suide Fhearghas. 'In pronouncing other Gaelic names the reader can do what I do—make a guess and hope for the best.'

Most of the names are descriptive of the terrain. I was bemused, when reading Mr Downie's list of local placenames at the variety of names for 'a little hill'—Am Binnein; Bennan, Cnocan, Torbeg (the last-named being explained as 'the little hill or bleaching green'). The old folk named other hills after a little gap, a vessel, a brown hue, a dappled appearance, a heifer and some fawns (a term now used for fallow, a red deer's offspring being a calf); We read that Largy Beg, Mor, Meadonach represent 'the little, big, middle hillside' respectively.

Journeying southwards from our bothy by Brodick Bay, we parked the car and struck inland, looking for graves—the Giant's Graves from which, according to Mr Downie had been taken 'large deposits of burnt bone broken into very small fragments, which had all the appearance of human bones burnt by cremation. Four arrowheads and three large flint knives or scrapers were also found, as well as small fragments of pottery...'

We soon discovered a possible cause of death—the hill! 'Half a mile' was the distance noted on the signpost. Half a mile, indeed! It seemed half a mile to the point where we climbed half a mile up a one-in-two slope, to face yet another half-mile to the gloomy clearing in a modern conifer forest where lay the old graves. Perhaps we should have taken a short cut.

Climbing the hill was a knee-racking experience. Fred began counting the steps, and for a quarter of an hour he muttered like some medieval monk at his prayers before announcing that we had negotiated 247 steps. 'It beats Whitby,' he remarked, thinking of the long flight from near the harbour to the parish church perched high on the west cliff. A peculiarity at Whitby is that the counter never has the same total twice!

Our Arran excursion ended at Brodick Castle. Here were treasures in wood, glass and metal. Here, too, we saw rows of faded deer heads—90 heads, all but one of them being from local stock. (I forget where the ninetieth head was procured.)

An old retainer of the Duke of Hamilton told us a story from the boyhood of Lord Ronald. He befriended a village lad, one of a family of ten, who invited his Lordship to a meal—a simple country meal. Lord Ronald in return invited the village lad to have a meal at the castle. When his family had assembled, he staggered into the dining room with a large tin of syrup that still bore the floury fingermarks of the cook. He placed the tin in the centre of the table. His mother protested. Lord Ronald said: 'I didn't want our hospitality to be any less than that I got at my friend's house.'

That night, an easterly wind rattled the window of my room. It did at least drown the snoring of the lady golfer in the next room.

2 AFTER YOU, MR MENDELSSOHN!
Iona and Staffa

Ron—Fred's brother—said he once knew a man who thought a Barber-Greene was a hairdresser, when nearly everyone else knows it is a tarmac-laying machine. Ron's observation was made as we motored from the ferry onto the island of Mull and encountered roadmen at work. A grating sound indicated where Ron's vehicle had struck rock-bottom. As we overtook the Barber-Greene it seemed to me like an antediluvian monster which had settled down to a spell of grazing.

It was a prosaic introduction to Mull. On the way across the Sound from Oban, Fred had been recalling a romantic interlude in the past. Feeling 'slack set up', he impulsively booked a place on a painting course held at the Big Hoose by a quiet shore at Carsaig. In his mind's eye, he recalled a sandy beach and a stupendous sea cliff; blobs of colour on rhododendrons in the garden and ferns growing from moss on ancient trees. It was all part of Fred's fantasy world, of course…

We motored to Bunessan in bright sunshine using the Mull equivalent of the M1, between dark droll conifers, with the twin turrets of Ben More gleaming after recent snowfalls. Long before the Big Bang was taken to mean reorganization in the City, Ben More blew its top with a bang that must have brought an echo from the moon. Looking at the snow-crusted hill, rising to 966 metres, it was not easy to think of the immense scale of the devastation in volcanic times, when displaced material settled as far away as Yorkshire.

The volcanic spasms ended some 45 to 50 million years ago. Mull was left with a wild and rocky landscape which, even today, is little known and holds more sheep and deer than people. The name Mull means 'mass of hill', a reference to Ben More, though what we see is merely the stump of an ancient hill.

As we motored by Loch Scridain, we were reminded of the violent past in the natural terracing originally formed by flowing lava. Much later, ice scoured the landscape, and not until it retreated did Mull separate from Morvern and become the third largest island in the Hebrides.

Fred noticed a raven being harried by two hooded crows. We watched the crows 'pin' the larger bird on the beach by their persistent diving. When the raven plucked up courage and lumbered into the air, the crows made several spectacular dives, coming to within a few feet of the hapless bird as it beat its way vigorously across the loch. We walked down the beach hoping that the tide had ebbed sufficiently for us to see beds of the native oyster. We found some shells, also an abundance of mussels, which accounted for the sleek and contented appearance of the local oystercatchers.

Ron turned the car on to a by-road which had grass growing up the middle (Fred's 'sump-cleaner'). Ron had not forgotten his brother's tales about Carsaig. We motored through a fawn-and-brown landscape for perhaps four miles. It was surely the wilderness experience that would provide a classic introduction to the Promised Land. The road dipped between tracts of moorland. We saw waterfalls, crags and conifers. Carsaig appeared as Fred had described it. Rhododendrons were in bloom, some of the blossom a vivid red. Palm trees stood in a walled garden bright with daffodils. We saw the Big Hoose, looking cool and tranquil. We heard a murmur (no more) from the sea and we beheld the immense cliff of Fred's memory.

The main road skirted the edge of Ardtun, a former busy crofting area, and passed a memorial to the person who wrote the hymn 'Morning has broken'. Then it dipped to Loch na Lathaich which, said Fred, means 'the Loch with the Dirty Bottom'. Away to the west were the islands of the Treshnish group, volcanic in origin, slabby and dark, like a task force of aircraft carriers lying at anchor. I looked for and promptly found—because it is a little detached from the main group—the distinctive form of Bac Mor, better known as 'The Dutchman's Cap', a lava cone encircled by a lava rim.

Bunessan, where we stayed, consisted of mainly white buildings grouped around the head of the loch. Our quarters were in a detached house, blue-slated, its walls painted white. The house was tucked into the edge of the moor and looked out over a salt-stained, gale-blasted hedge, to the crescent shore of the loch. An incongruous feature beside the road was street lighting on tall concrete posts. The one near the house had perching space on top for two herring gulls, standing close together, side by side. Our neighbours included herons and curlews.

We met Tabby, a cat in the custody of a local lady who told us the creature was born in Belgium, had visited America, was currently a resident on a Scottish island and might soon be consigned to Australia, where its master and family now lived. The cat had spent about half its life in quarantine!

The wind was from the north, so we took to the lee shore, reached by a cul de sac from Bunessan. The sand was unblemished by human foot or tractor tyre. At one of the innumerable Hebridean 'deserted villages', someone had left a building partly roofed, which served us well as a passing cloud disgorged hail. Whooper swans sailed on Loch Assapool; the local hooded crows harried a buzzard and two ravens passed over with gruff calls, as though swearing at the crows.

Fresh snow had fallen on Ben More: we saw the top of the hill gleaming whiter than white as the sunshine reached it. The northern wind gathered the fine, hard snow, which cascaded down the southern side in a spectacular avalanche.

The old crofting area of Ardtun looked as though its best days were over. The road we used to reach it was overgrown, and everywhere signs of neglect were not hard to find. But where a family remained true to the land, the old feeling of pride was apparent. At one croft, there was some banter about the wee wifie's dilemma. Expecting another child, she had not been aware of being pregnant until Hogmanay, five months later. Yet she had been giving her husband a hand moving sacks of potatoes from sodden fields!

An impromptu meal was organised, Fred producing half a bottle of whisky and the crofter's wife a plate of ham sandwiches and biscuits. We heard of the iniquities of the hooded crow and of how, one spring, the crofter caught 27 'whoodies', using a type of trap recommended by the Forestry Commission—a frame with netting, entry being gained through a funnel. It was virtually impossible for a crow to return the same way. We were told of otters that had attacked domestic ducks, of adders that were relatively common on the moors and of the lizards that had their lodgings in a local wall.

On Easter Sunday I decided to go to church—on Iona. I was delivered to the ferry and noticed with amusement that the ferryman was keeping banknotes in his hand and coins in a biscuit tin. It was an overcast, chilly morning. Tide and wind fought it out in the Sound. Then, as we waited to enter the Abbey, the wind fought us. A young man with a beard, a dark donkey jacket and bright red slacks, told us of the arrangements for the service. We rehearsed two simple songs. We collected the order of service, which had been duplicated on daffodil-yellow paper.

On May 12, 563, Iona became a spiritual power-house of European importance when Columba and twelve of his brethren arrived by coracle from the Derry coast—and, turning their backs on Ireland, pondered on the tasks they must perform for Christ in a heathen land. They are said to have symbolically buried their coracle, but there would have been a local need for it. The gentle Celtic monks moved restlessly from island to island, from headland to headland, from pagan kingdom to pagan kingdom, at the western fringe of the Continent. They helped to maintain the light of reason and religion in dark times.

Long before I visited Iona, my imagination had been fired by tales of the early Celtic Church. I pictured Columba and his monks occupying a grey rock in a grey sea; they would either be sleeping in their rock cells or praying with their eyes fixed heavenwards. I never thought of such down-to earth activities as food-hunting, eating and washing. The reality was at first disappointing. From Fionnphort I beheld a relatively large, fertile island, quite close to Mull. It has been tripperish for years, the trippers ranging from those on pilgrimage, their eyes fixed on the Abbey, to holidaymakers who visit Iona because it's there—and because going there is one of the excursions they have paid for!

Wordsworth, visiting Iona in 1833, was irritated by the tourist throng:

> We saw but surely, in that motley crowd,
> Not one of us has felt the far-famed sight;
> How could we feel it? each the other's blight,
> Hurried and hurrying, volatile and loud.

What happened to Columba's shrine we do not know: it is said to have been moved to Ireland when the Norsemen were active along the coast. The story of a succession of religious buildings on a sacred site makes stirring reading, but for me it was sufficient to know that what remained was given by the Duke of Argyll to the Church of Scotland, and that in due course an Iona Community was established, inspired by the Rev George MacLeod, and the buildings were restored. A religious community maintains the fabric and invests it with a true Christian spirit.

That Easter Sunday morning, we formed a ragged throng. There was not much formality: we did not progress in a crocodile, neither were the worshipers attired in Sunday best. Each wore layers of warm clothing, with a variety of headgear, including knitted caps, and a variety of footwear, including big boots and wellies.

The altar was adorned with a poster-type message: JESUS RULES OK. Flags had been strung along the choir stalls. Columba is said to have detested women and to have banished them to an island off Iona. Now, 1,400 years later, a young girl preached a simple, purposeful sermon. It was topical, too, with its references to redundant workers, nuclear warfare and sufferers from strife in South America. Musically, the service was outstanding. For some lyrical items, piano and flute provided an irresistible combination.

At the Sharing of the Bread and Wine, the celebrant stood with others behind the altar and the bread was taken round by children. The person at the end of a row took a piece, broke off a portion to eat, and passed the rest on. The wine was distributed with a similar lack of formality: large jug-like containers were passed from hand to hand down the rows. A processional hymn began with the appearance of a young man carrying a large cross decked with daffodils, followed by two young people holding banners. The procession led to the Cloisters, where tea was provided for the now chilled company—for there was no heating in the building.

At Fionnphort, I had given my name to the boatman who organised trips to Staffa. But then the weather deteriorated, with a fall of snow. When the boat came over from Iona I was told that the party who had booked no longer wanted to cross seven or eight miles of open sea to Fingal's Cave. On that chilly, snowy, misty afternoon, who could blame them?

It was disappointing, nonetheless. When I was a small boy, receiving a penny on alternate Saturdays, I managed to save enough money (with birthday gifts) to buy a gramophone record. That was long before such a thing was called a 'disc'. Each Saturday morning, I took the record to the home of an old lady who had a good quality gramophone, and she allowed me to play it. That record was the Hebrides Overture, or 'Fingal's Cave', inspired by a visit which Felix Mendelssohn made to Staffa in 1829. Sir Walter Scott had been there in 1810, John Keats in 1818, and after Mendelssohn came the artist Turner in 1830, Wordsworth, Queen Victoria and Prince Albert in 1833. Jules Verne, who sailed to Fingal's Cave in 1859, wrote about it in a book, The Green Ray, which was published in 1885.

Next morning, with the weather clear and calm, I rang up the boatman. He would not be sailing to Staffa, he said, because he had not succeeded in interesting anyone else in the venture. I asked him how much it would cost me to hire his boat. 'Fifty pounds,' he said, which was not unreasonable from his point of view. As for me, I had thought of £20; perhaps—if pushed—£30. 'Thirty-five pounds,' he said. The call of Staffa was strong; it had haunted my dreams since boyhood. It was just a few miles away. 'Thirty pounds,' I heard myself replying. 'Right. I'll pick you up at 10.30.'

He kept his boat in a sheltered spot called the Bull Hole. As I waited for the craft to arrive, I thought of Mendelssohn, who came to London, was thrilled by the bustle and cosmopolitan clamour and then had a holiday in Scotland, being especially moved by the storm-racked seas of the Hebrides.

He and a friend toured the Highlands long before tourism had developed. He wrote:

To describe the wretchedness and comfortless inhospitable solitude of the country here, time and space do not allow me. We wandered 10 days without seeing a single traveller. What are marked on the map as towns or at least villages are just a few sheds huddled together, with one and the same hole for door, window and chimney, for the exit of men, animals, light and smoke... And even such inhabited spots are but sparingly scattered over the country. The roads are deserted.

It is no wonder that the Highlands have been called 'melancholy'. But two fellows have wandered through them, laughed at every opportunity, rhymed and sketched together, growled at one another and at the world if they happened to be vexed or found nothing to eat, devoured everything in sight when they did find it and slept 12 hours every night. These two were we—and we'll not forget it as long as we live.

The boat I hired had a crew of two, the owner's assistant being a young man with a black beard and a cheerful disposition that belied his dark appearance. We sailed northwards, with Staffa in view the whole time. No 'white tops' were revealed; the sea had an awesome swell; which surprised me, for it was a day when a procession of short, sharp storms swept in from the sea and ran amok inland, bombarding the hills with hail. The storms were of a local nature; the swell probably began 1,000 miles or so away, in the midst of nowhere, and was only now encountering the land.

The swell as it affects the Hebrides was described by the eighth Duke of Argyll, on a visit to Tiree. When no wind blew, when the surface of the sea was as calm as the surface of glass or oil, he saw 'vast undulations, in which acres of water were in movement and which advanced with a silent, majestic motion... On meeting shallows, still more in encountering rocks, they at once rose in threatening and rapidly advancing crests, and then broke in furious foam and surge.'

Off our port bow were the Treshnish Islands, notably the Dutchman's Cap. I heard from the boatman how a crofter living on Iona hired the craft for a day at a time when he intended to transport sheep to the islands or to bring them back just before the autumn sales. The Dutchman has a broad brim on which cattle were once summered. The vegetation was so poor that only 19 cattle were taken across by boat; it was said that 'twenty would starve'.

A few guillemots went by like feathered darts, working their small wings so quickly they were blurred to human vision. Manx shearwaters were in more leisurely flight, gliding mainly, using the uprush of air from the heaving sea.

One advantage of hiring a boat was that I could spread myself without ceaseless apologies. Mainly, I looked ahead, and saw Staffa resolve itself from a dark blob to a row of basalt pillars, 60 feet high. Mendelssohn was only 19 years old when he came to Staffa, and he put his impressions directly into musical notes, scribbled in a letter he wrote to his sister. Later he would refer to his 'misty Scottish mood'. His companion, Klingemann, used words: a greener roar of waves never rushed into a stranger cavern, 'its many pillars making it look like the inside of an immense organ, black and resounding and absolutely without purpose, and quite alone, the wide grey sea within and without.'

Now I was close to Fingal's Cave, I was trying to match Mendelssohn's music as it ran through my brain to the flurry of salt water and the swirling gulls. From a distance, the pillars had seemed like an over-generous filling in a geological sandwich, but now they dominated the view, framed by worn rocks. The pillars were not vertical; the tilt of the basalt bed gave the impression that Staffa was about to slip under water.

We lay off the island, taking the wild sea astern. With Staffa close by, I marvelled that life had once been possible here. The name is said to be derived from a Norse word for 'post', after the wooden posts used for house-building. Why not from the basalt pillars? The cave is named after Fionn MacCaul, the Celtic giant who, when he was not busy here, was building the Giant's Causeway on the Antrim coast. I liked Klingemann's comparison with an organ; the Gaelic name, *An Uamh Binn*, is translated as 'the melodious cave'.

With Staffa close by, the sea was no longer just a green corrugation; it exploded against islets, skerries and against Staffa itself. White water, like some marine geyser, broke to a height of around 50 feet. Our presence disturbed a large flock of grey geese. The boatman mentioned the puffins that nest on the north of the island. Fulmars were on patrol, and in the lee of Staffa we came under the scrutiny of a grey seal.

The boatman circumnavigated the island, as compensation for not being able to land upon it; he knew when to steer well out to avoid hitting rocks that do not quite break surface. We ran into the wind, and the boat slammed against the sea. The swell burst against skerries, clouding the air with fine spray. It must have been on such a day that Mendelssohn was here.

That, at least, is how the music of 'Fingal's Cave' strikes you—and has struck me down many years. Later, I began to hear other ideas about the genesis of that famous Overture—of how Mendelssohn, overcome by seasickness, lay down below, listening not to the roar of waves against the rocks but the throb of the piston of the *Highlander*, the small steamer which conveyed' visitors from Oban to Staffa. The composer, swaddled in blankets, nauseated by the smell of onions being cooked in the galley, stayed on board the ship. It was his companion, Klingemann, who alighted on the dark rocks and, clambering up to the basaltic columns beside Fingal's Cave, yelled with the sheer joy of being alive in such an impressive place.

I was put ashore on Iona, and after ordering haddock and chips in a steamed-up-restaurant I had not previously noticed, I returned to Mull and to a welling up of island fever as I thought of Robert Louis Stevenson, author of *Treasure Island*. He stayed on Erraid while he wrote a major part of *Kidnapped*. Erraid lies about four miles south of Fionnphort and can be reached across sand and rocks when the tide is out.

I decided to rejoin Fred and Ron at Bunessan and cadged a lift in a dormobile belonging to a couple from Cheshire who had been coming to these parts for 20 years. They bought some prawns from the trawlers visiting Bunessan pier. Some years ago, this delightful couple were in the area when they saw the Royal yacht appear, drop anchor and, while a destroyer patrolled farther out, the Queen and her family were brought ashore for a picnic.

Fred, Ron and I explored the Ardtun peninsula. We found ourselves in a strange world of columnar basalt, all of it curved, some in a form that reminded us of the beams of a Viking longship. The cliffs were high; the gulleys deep, enough to have attracted some nesting shags, which sat on their soggy, compost-like nests and screeched at us—an echo from prehistory. We heard a sound like a demented woodpecker: it was a geology student, wielding a hammer, bashing away at the 'leaf' beds that formed some so million years ago—before the volcanic activity had begun. The lad was continuing a slow, natural process that would one day undercut the cliff and lead to its collapse.

We had the sad experience of finding the remains of a butt and ben dwelling, with a rusted sewing machine lying outside, close to an old horse plough. Within an area colonised by bramble and dock, pieces of iron from the old fireplace reclined. Daffodils flowered within the tangle of a walled garden run to seed. It was only human to ponder the life the family had led.

We heard of a family who moved from house to house as each building reached a stage when it was about to collapse. The owners then took up residence in a caravan.

On our last evening, we enjoyed a real Hebridean sunset. At about eight o'clock, the hue in the western sky changed from lemon to pink. The few clouds were empurpled as the sky and the sea were tinted red. It looked as though the clouds were bleeding. Fred glanced at snow-capped Ben More by moonlight, and said: 'Pity we had to have Christmas at Easter.'

3 PLENTY OF PUFFINS
The Treshnish Islands

We stood in the rain near Ulva Ferry, in the far west of Mull, having walked from Salen along the northern shore of Loch na Keal. The rain shower had arrived from who-knows-where as we looked around for a likely dining table. The most promising object was a wooden pallet that had recently held bags of fertiliser. On it we spread our simple fare: baps and butter, beef and cheese, one Coke and two bottles of Perrier water. A plastic knife was our sole item of cutlery.

We dined to music provided by the local skylark and with an improving view across the sound to Ulva island, beyond which, our map told us, lay the Treshnish Islands a scattering of volcanic rocks, from assorted skerries to the big stuff—Lunga (isle of puffins) and the Dutchman's Cap.

It was May. Benign nature had put a film of blue in the woods and peppered the gorse with gold. Waders nesting along the shore maintained an effective early warning system of sharp eyes and ears. The shoreline echoes were roused by the 'kleep' of the oystercatcher, the brisk trill of the sandpiper, a soft purring from the ringed plover and the honking of a testy crow.

It was while looking at an oystercatcher as it stood sentinel on a rock near the breaking waves that I noticed the otters: two lithesome creatures working their way along the shore, negotiating rocks, entering clear pools, making brief sorties on the loch and returning to push their way through a tangle of weed.

Their actions formed one continuing graceful movement, almost without pause. When an otter was afloat it kept low in the water, showing the top of its head, the hump of the body and a long, stiff tail. One of them, making tunnels in the weed, was garlanded with the stuff when it raised itself on its hind legs and peered around.

The two otters performed many actions as one. Together they swam into the loch for perhaps 20 yards, dived and returned to the surface with crabs which were brought ashore to some flat rocks. Here they crunched the shells and claws to reach the nourishing flesh. The indigestible items were left littering the rocks.

From a range of about ten yards, I peered through my binoculars at their whiskered faces. An otter has a fine sense of smell but its eyesight is not particularly keen. Fred recalled being told in Tobermory of the local otter that was hand-fed by visitors on potato crisps. The lochside otters sat manoeuvring crabs with their forepaws. The longer they were out of the water, the drier did their pelage become, so that detail emerged on what had been a smooth brown coat. Eventually they departed by water, swimming side by side.

At Tobermory, after a substantial meal that did not include crabs, we strolled along the prom, teasing (and being teased by) the fishermen, marvelling yet again at the multicoloured buildings, doubly colourful when they were reflected in the calm water. The harbour itself demanded to be noticed. The mouth of the bay is almost blocked by Calve Island, which breaks the back of any wild sea, offering the fisherman and the yachtsman a safe anchorage within the bay. Visitors who have read the guide books look across the bay, half expecting to see the rotting masts and spars of a galleon of the Spanish Armada which foundered here in 1588. The Spaniards had assisted a MacLean to ravage a kinsman's estates on Coll; MacLean then demanded blackmail money from the Spanish captain, and he refused. So two Scotsmen went aboard and fired the magazine. The shattered galleon sank in eleven fathoms and the wreck is now believed to lie below many feet of clay, but she lives on under full sail as an illustration in books, on T-shirts, tea towels—and the napkins at one of the eating places we patronised.

Next day we met the owner of the Treshnish Isles. As we took the path to Haunn, we chatted briefly with Lady Jean Rankin, of Treshnish House. She was for some years Lady-in-Waiting to the Queen Mother. Our walk continued along the edge of moorland to cottages where lobster fishermen once lived. Breaking the western horizon were some of the Treshnish group of islands, formed when the sea cut back the edges of ancient lava flows. The sight of the blue Islands reinforced our desire to visit them.

First, however, we must see the grandeur of western Mull, with its green-step landscape and precipitous cliffs. We strode on terraces created by the weathering of Tertiary basalt, the underlying rock of much of this big island. A few sheep picked their way across a landscape which was once able to maintain a large stock of cattle. It was the coming of many sheep and the attendant burning of the rough grass the kine had eaten, that robbed Mull of much of its ancient fertility.

A well-used path led to the shore. The cliffs had the dull red appearance of firebricks. An awesome stack was tufty with red (thrift), white (campion) and blue (the ubiquitous bluebell). Everywhere, cock wheatears displayed, taking short flights and uttering creaky calls.

The cliffs had been under-cut. The driest and least conspicuous of the caves had been used for the illegal distilling of whisky until a new law proclaimed that owners of the land on which a still was found would be considered as guilty as the distillers themselves. That scared the local gentry. Local guide books mention The Still Cave, with its turf wall reared along the front, to shield the furnace glow from any passing vessel. The needs of the islanders were soon met. In far-off times, many a run of spirits ended on the Irish coast.

We snoozed away the hour of noon and, moving inland, found the substantial remains of roofless blackhouses of the pre-nineteenth-century type, built without chimneys. The trickle of water nearby was scarcely adequate to earn it the term 'burn', but it had at least made life practicable for a community between the moors and the salty sea. It appears that land was cultivated in common. We were still speculating about the origin and use of a pond when we regained the road and our car.

That evening, after a meal at one of the harbourside restaurants of Tobermory, my ambition to visit the Treshnish group of islands came a stage nearer. We chatted with some of the fishermen, who related tales of the isles, including how— about seven years before—14 bullocks had been turned on the Dutchman's Cap to graze. At summer's ending, only 12 beasts could be caught. The remaining two wandered across the island in a semi-wild state, each weighing about one and a-half tons, itself a deterrent to those with ambitions to recapture them.

One of the lobster men offered me a place on the boat the following morning at 6 a.m. I set my watch-alarm for 5 a.m., only to be awakened by someone else's watch-alarm which had been set for 4.45 a.m. The sun—a red orb—cleared the horizon at 5.30. I was at the harbourside by 5.50.

Cameron and David were already busy on the boat which had a deck house forrard, with plenty of open space on which to attend to the lobster pots, known hereabouts as 'creels'. Cameron, at the wheel, was surrounded by much electronic wizardry. David busied himself in the timeless task of cutting up bait-mackerel, packed in a metal drum. He then prepared the first of several cups of coffee.

On the run out to the lobstering grounds, there was little to do except talk. The echo-sounder revealed that we had 12 fathoms under the keel and that the bed of the sea was mud. One would not expect to find lobsters there. The outline of the coast showed as a silvery doodle on the radar screen. To the north lay Ardnamurchan, a finger of rock intent on tickling the ribs of the Western Isles. I was reminded that this is the most westerly point on the British mainland—some 20 miles west of Land's End.

In Calgary Bay, we operated just off the rocks while the first tourist visitors of the day strode along the shell-sand beach, a rarity on Mull's western coast. The sands formed a smooth white crescent, beyond which lay the fresh green of the machair and well-wooded hills. According to John Prebble, the enduring myth should be true—that the emigrants who left their homes at Calgary, on the white shore of Mull, gave its name to a new settlement, Calgary in Alberta. In fact, it was named by a policeman in 1876 and was intended to be a compliment to his relation by marriage, the laird of Calgary on Mull.

Cameron remarked, 'Don't worry if we stroke the rocks. We're right into the keel here.' David used a grappling iron to collect the rope which, marked by buoys, indicated where the 'fleet' of lobster creels lay. Cameron used a small winch to get them aboard. Each creel was set on the gunwale, its contents being briefly and excitedly examined. One never knows what a creel will contain...

Big lobsters were retained for sale, and most of them would be consigned to France; medium-sized lobsters were checked against a metal gauge and, if found wanting, were dropped over the side. Large crabs were tossed back, except for some choice specimens which were boiled for 20 minutes. Mixed with mayonnaise, the crab meat provided us with tasty sandwiches as we voyaged between the coast of Mull and the islands. 'Velvet crabs'—the top of the shell had a velvety feel—were retained. 'The Spaniards are keen on them.'

Some thinking time was possible as we furrowed the sea towards the islands. The Treshnish group first came to my attention in the early part of the 1939–45 war, with the publication of Frank Fraser Darling's *Island Years*. Quite apart from the joy in reading of scientific work carried out in the field rather than in some musty laboratory, there was the sheer excitement of the prose. The author was ceaselessly on the move. He had a crisp and economical style that was like opening a window to admit a sea breeze.

I met Darling only once, and was tongue-tied in the presence of a man I greatly admired. He spoke to me! We were having a snack meal during a British Deer Society gathering in Perth. He leaned from his table towards mine and asked, 'May I parasitise you?' He wanted to borrow the sugar basin!

In the book, he concentrated on how he and his family lived during his Island Years. For part of the time they were on Lunga, the largest of the Treshnish group. They were put ashore from a cruiser on to weed-covered rocks, and found themselves on a green but rabbit-infested island.

On my lobstering trip, we had no time to go ashore, though Cameron took the boat close in to the rocks, where the best lobster ground was found. David fed the creels over the side in a way that did not snag the heap of rope. The retained lobsters, which had been dispersed to avoid fighting, were attended to and then David, using a hosepipe, cleared the deck of its accumulated weed and creatures such as starfish and sea-urchins. The herring gulls fluttering in our wake gobbled down what took their fancy.

I ate a crab sandwich. 'You'll know when you've had enough,' said David. 'You'll start walking sideways.' We reset our course, had more cups of coffee and spread on well-buttered cream crackers any crab meat that remained.

The biggest lobsters were drawn up from beside the skerries, where salt water slopped over weed-strewn rocks and the greater black-backed gulls stood in mournful contemplation of the sea. Fulmar petrels, when disturbed by the approach of the boat, took flight with pattering feet.

Lobstering was resumed among the dark rocks off the northernmost islets of the Treshnish group. The routine was the same—haul, collect, re-bait, re-lay the creels, tossing overboard the marker buoys. At one point we were off the west of Fladda with ten fathoms of water beneath us; 'Aboutfour cups in the kettle,' said David. Another boat appeared. Its young owner had not fared well that day. Cameron, thinking of recent days, said, 'He's been doing fine for the wee boat he has.'

When he had departed, Cameron announced, 'We'll go through the gap.' He was referring to a minor channel between an islet and a skerry. We almost brushed the rocks. For a few seconds, even the watchful gulls stopped breathing.

The local lobsters included some five-pounders. We loitered between the Treshnish Isles in the company of black guillemots and eiders. Cameron performed daring deeds in wild water or ventured into the shallows. As he did three jobs at once, not least controlling the boat, I looked down to a forest of kelp, the fronds of which moved under the influence of unseen currents. There did not seem to be enough water to float a plastic duck. The boat was then nudged into deeper water, using a combination of engine and tidal pull. Cameron looked pleased. 'We had 18 lobsters in that fleet,' he said. Each creel was stripped of its accumulated kelp, given fresh bait and stacked in the stern. 'Our creels are metal-framed, covered in plastic. They're made down in Yorkshire—at Dewsbury.'

Grey seals, awoken from their slumbers by the engine's lusty roar, reared their heads and tails until they were shaped like bananas, and languidly watched us go by. A bull seal preferred to watch while 'treading' water. Out here, where the sea bloomed and there was food for all, our catch became more varied.

We still had lobsters and velvet crabs, but one creel held a dog whelk, another a rockling and a third a dogfish, which resembled a miniature shark. These non-commercial creatures were returned to the sea.

At the south-eastern side of Lunga, with the cliffs and dark scars never far away, the sea boiled as half a dozen eager currents fought for supremacy. The creels we took in were almost twice as large as the others and demanded more effort to collect, re-bait and return. A score of fulmars assembled on the fretful sea, looking for food. One of our attendant herring gulls wore several plastic identity rings on its legs.

During one haul I let my eyes range over Lunga's bird-haunted cliffs. Fulmars croaked and displayed; razorbills stood looking immaculate in their dark 'jackets' and white 'fronts'. Just above where the waves broke stood nesting shags: they occupied deep ledges or small caves, their coarse voices mingling with the croaking of fulmars to produce a medley that seemed half as old as time.

A startled octopus was tipped from one creel. It looked pale—like an uncooked haggis with legs. Minutes later, it had become a browny-red. Cameron said: 'It's not too keen on being caught!'

The last haul was in the lee of Lunga. Waves broke against Harp Rock with a dull thud and a sheet of Daz-white spray. Auks thronged the air like bees around a hive. The sea held rafts of guillemots, with a scattering of puffins. At our approach, they were not sure whether to dive or fly. To take to the air, a guillemot had to work its wings furiously, its feet pattering on the waves. The wings whirred like some freshly-wound clockwork device that becomes blurred to human vision.

Panic spread through the ranks as an avian buccaneer—the Arctic skua—swept into view. Fixing its attention on some luckless gull, it harried the bird with such determination that it parted with the contents of its crop, which was precisely what the skua intended. Food that should have nourished a gull now vanished into the digestive system of the skua. A common skua, known in northern Scotland as the 'bonxie', had been seen off the Treshnish Islands...

With 101 lobsters on board, and all the creels attended to, Cameron set a homeward course. He pointed out the outcropping rocks which, from a distance, give the impression of a surfacing submarine. Near Tobermory, lobsters and crabs were put in a special container and lowered into the sea to keep them alive until they could be taken by tanker to the French market. Early next morning, Cameron and David would return to the Treshnish Isles this time to the Dutchman's Cap, and then to haul fleets of creels off Ardnamurchan. 'It will be a longer day.'

Having been to Lunga, I could re-read Fraser Darling's book with special interest. I envied the scientist his spell there—his encounters with Manx shearwaters, and hearing the churnng sound made by storm petrels in the walls of old houses and under boulders near where the tents had been pitched.

Having been out with the modern lobster fishermen, who have all the latest scientific aids to navigation and echo-sounding, I was fascinated by an account of the Robertson family, who not only lifted lobsters from around these islands but lived in a small hut on Fladda each summer, returning to Tobermory for the winter to attend to their equipment and make it ready for another season.

I also envied the Darling party its opportunities to watch grey seals, including Old Tawny, a bull seal about ten feet long and weighing perhaps 700 pounds. The seal was stalked to such close range that Darling could see his powerful 'hand' with its five black claws. 'He rumbled inside and the very rock seemed to shake...'

Fred and Ron returned from an excursion to the isles with stirring tales of puffins.

One fretful bird had nipped Ron's shoe. They had been amused to see that some burrows were interchangeable as dwellings between rabbits and puffins. Intrigued by flurries of loose soil spurting from a burrow, they had watched as a puffin emerged to scan them from a range of five feet.

George and I sailed from Ulva Ferry to Lunga in a fiberglass boat that was at home in the tidal rips. As we cleared the sound, a sneaky wind ruffled the sea and also the clothes of those who, minutes before, had joyously claimed the rear seats. The first fine curtain of spray brought a taste of salt to our lips. By keeping close to the cliffs of Ulva, we found stretches of calm water.

It was gloomy against the cliffs: a television production of the voyage would certainly have included strains by Wagner. Shags which had built their weedy nests on what were obscure ledges now had waterborne humans peering at them from a range of a few feet. Grey seals had settled down to rest on lonely promontories and were now under the scrutiny of excited visitors.

We crossed the gunmetal-grey sea to Staffa. A fellow passenger said, 'looking at that big cave makes you want to yawn!' Yet a monk of Iona, who settled by Lake Zurich in Switzerland, founded a settlement he called Stafa, after the Hebridean island. Joseph Banks, President of the Royal Society, while voyaging to Iceland in the summer of 1772, thought he had discovered the island, and those around him did nothing to correct him.

Our boatman circumnavigated the island, keeping as near as he dared to the unseen reefs that suddenly produced geyser-like jets of white water. An old lady who was interested in the Dutchman's Cap explained that she came from Holland. We discussed Hebridean associations with Dutchmen. Maybe the name Dutchman's Cap comes from those Dutch fishermen of two centuries ago who were among the first to turn herring fishing into big business. The island would have been a major navigational feature.

Our boat slipped into a sheltered mooring between black rocks on Lunga. Nesting herring gulls shouted a protest as we crossed the area of grey rock and pockets of grass where their nests were situated. We sat among the puffins that had entranced Fred and Ron.

George said the puffins reminded him of portly aldermen who had attended some civic function. Their small, squat forms, with the black and white of 'evening dress', certainly lived up to an impression of aldermen, and perhaps George imagined that the flattened beak, with its stripes of red, suggested they had imbibed too freely and had inflamed noses.

The puffins stood looking at us, or—if we were near their nesting burrows—approached to within a few inches, as though suggesting that we move on. One bird leaned forward, peering intently into a burrow as though expecting a rabbit to pop out.

Puffins are most plentiful on islands with well-broken shorelines. Beyond one gully, the birds were nesting among rocks and using large boulders as perches. More puffins arrived with whirring wings; they displayed to each other or wandered about with dry grass in their beaks. One puffin slept away the early afternoon, its body resting on the ground and its neck bent so that the triangular beak could be buried under a scapular.

In the same rocky area, shags had found secluded places and would have been overlooked but for the profusion of droppings, forming whitewashed areas, and their rasping calls whenever we walked near. A shag on its untidy, soggy nest raised its head crest, swayed its neck and croaked as though it was ripping the sides of its throat.

Harp Rock, seen from the landward side, was truly impressive, for it was half-covered with crouching guillemots. Their growling, and the rousing calls of the kittiwakes, created the familiar basic sound of a seabird colony; the musty smell was there, too, and I heard the slap of waves against smooth rock and the pounding of water beyond. The guillemots on Harp Rock were protecting their eggs by sheer force of numbers from the predatory herring gulls. Crouched side by side, nose to tail, they feathered the otherwise naked rock, each bird clinging to the nestless egg as it would later clasp its downy young. To relax the grip was to invite disaster, in the form of an attack from a vigilant gull or premature death following a tumble into the sea. The razorbills, thinly scattered and nesting in cracks and crannies, were less vulnerable. Seventy per cent of the world's razorbills nest on the islands of Britain.

We reversed from the channel between waves and soon gained the safety of open water.

4 EASTER ON THE BENS
Crianlarich

Every expedition should have an objective. On this trip, it was to taste a capercaillie sandwich. Our largest game bird had been seen in a local wood and reported in the press. We did not see a caper, and had to be content with Fred's story of how he once had capercaillie and chips, but we found yet another 'window' in the weather and walked in a hard northern sunlight which brought out the russet tones of the glens and gave the snow-capped bens a resemblance to ice-cream cornets. As the week went by, the snow on the hills diminished visibly: we were presumably carrying it away on our boots!

At our selected guest-house, mine host donned a kilt and stuck a dirk in his starboard sock, for the serving of meals. We met two jovial lads who were employed to drive refrigerated trucks around Scotland, distributing sausages and bacon. It would cost one of the companies £84 for a short sea passage for the van, a surcharge of five per cent being made to cover the extra cost of the journey.

Although the caper eluded us, I awoke on the first morning to the cooing and hissing of demonstrative blackcock on the lek. Looking across a tract of rough ground newly planted with trees, I saw two birds facing each other, with drooping wings and frilly undertail-coverts as they went through the age-old quest for a female, the 'greyhen', seeking to reach and hold the dominant part of the lekking ground, which she would visit in due course.

We motored through Tyndrum, which is like a mid-West staging post, with a wild setting. Before reaching the even wilder moor of Rannoch, we turned off to park the car and walk under the railway viaduct in the shadow of Beinn Dorain. Our track, which glistened with mica, kept such close company with the burn that we crossed the water a dozen times. Then, pausing on hearing a strident sound, we watched open-mouthed as two men on Japanese motorbikes shattered the ageless peace of the hills. The men were from Paisley; they had ridden up-country to fish the hill lochs.

We overtook another angler to whom all non-Scottish folk were 'bloody'. He told us aggressively that 'bloody Yorkshiremen are always talking about brass'. He'd no time for 'bloody landowners', especially foreigners. John threw in a verbal hand-grenade by asking him if he was a Scottish Nationalist. The man stopped in mid-sentence, then said, 'I just love the place.' After that, he became quite friendly. We discovered that the local hills 'are kinda smooth for eagles'. We should see a buzzard—'and lots of bloody crows'.

A cock wheatear welcomed us to the hill country. The bird chacked and whistled in its territory among the boulders. Meadow pipits showed off in the sunshine, descending in their celebrated 'shuttlecock' flight, with wings and tail feathers held stiffly outwards.

We crossed the watershed—there was, indeed, a shed, of wood and corrugated iron!—and descended to Loch Lyon, pausing only to pick up the sun-bleached skull of a sheep and place it on a boulder, where it looked like a prop in a Western movie. Fred consulted his new pedometer (which became known as a Fredometer) and announced that we had covered 6.85 miles: So we settled on a handy beach and ate our packed meal. We looked across the water at a wee cottage, truly a remote place, where the shepherd would spend two or three weeks during the lambing season.

We wondered if such dedicated workers could be found today.

It was John who first commented on the numerous lively frogs—all stimulated into action by the lengthening days and the spring warmth. There were frogs in the glens and in moist drainage channels at over 1,000 feet; everywhere amorous frogs were doing what came naturally. Frog spawn had been deposited wherever there was water, and much of it would dry out when the shallows evaporated in the heat of the afternoon sun. Bountiful nature ensured that the frog population of these parts would at least be sustained. The water rippled as frogs went under cover of weed or rocks; other frogs simply froze, with retracted undercarriages. Fred told us, with all the authority of one who had just read a Reader's Digest book on wildlife, that the amorous male grows special appendages on its legs so that it can hold on to a female.

We strode back to the car. Fred's pedometer had recorded 13 miles, John's registered 14 miles. We speculated on various aspects of that day's jaunt—and then decided that henceforth the highest of the two figures would count!

After dinner, we walked a mile or two into the village for drinks. I overheard someone talking about a haggis being 'headed and knotted'. On the return, our revellers saw stars—real stars. Fred and John star-gazed through binoculars but could not hold them steady enough, with the result that Jupiter dashed madly about the night sky trailing a silver tail. Fred pointed out his favourite stars which he named Accles and Pollock.

Next morning, the sun rose on a frosted countryside. I went for a walk, and saw blackcock and greyhen, raven, red grouse and buzzard. From the sky came the curious bleating sound produced when a snipe dives in the sharp air with its stiffened outer tail feathers extended. A robin sang high on a birch tree—as robins have undoubtedly done since birds colonised the post-glacial wilderness.

Glencoe awaited us. We crossed the ragged moor of Rannoch and paused at the roadside to watch skiers on Meall a Bhuiridh. One poor wretch, when halfway down, appeared to have lost his nerve. Our binoculared gaze allowed us to see him taking off his skis. He seemed intent on walking the rest of the way!

The car park offered an undisturbed view of the Buckle (Buchaille Etive Mor). It was a relief to turn our back on it and, instead to follow the zig-zags of General Wade's military road—also known as the Devil's Staircase—gaining 700 feet in a distance of one-and-a-half miles. Fred pitied any soldier who was commanded to carry some cannon balls.

We were still alive, though in no mood for kicking, when the road levelled out and began its shallow descent to Kinlochleven. Beyond the brown-and-orange countryside rose Ben Nevis, the attic of Britain. Needless to say, it was snow-capped. We were pleased to see it, though many another hill· in the district was more shapely than the 1,361 m (4,406 ft) slab of granite. (Wainwright told me he rated Glen Nevis, at the foot of the mountain, as the most beautiful glen in Scotland.)

We climbed to an elevation of about 3,000 feet and looked from A Chailleach towards Ambodach. Far below us, in Glencoe, early visitors were enjoying the sensations of spring; up here it was still winter, with white cornices attached to the ridge.

We had the somewhat crazy idea of following the path along the summits of Aonach Eagach and sensibly elected to scramble down into Glencoe. It was sensible only because we avoided the ridge. The unstable path lay through a gully, beside the creaming waters of a burn, and we needed the nerves of goats. Some lads who had negotiated the famous Aonach Eagach still had the energy to bound down the slope. Ron wistfully recalled that, when he was young, he always ran up hills.

We slithered and grunted our way into the glen. For a time we could follow the old road, on a carpet of short, springy turf, with the company of wheatears. 'I reckon the sheep keep this road in good condition,' said Fred. Then, with regret, we reached the modern road, on which—surely—it would be possible to land a Boeing 707. For half an hour we had the whine and whoosh of speeding traffic to distract us from Glencoe, where echoes of the seventeenth-century massacre still linger and the valley is known as the Glen of Weeping.

Venturing from Crianlarich into an area of Scots pines, we admired the bottle-green foliage against the orangy bark of trunk and branches. The local landowner had fenced off 30 acres to give nature a chance, but elsewhere the sheep prevented any natural regeneration of timber. And in another area, the delicate coverlet of peat and soil over glacial clay—a coverlet painstakingly built up over thousands of years—had been ripped asunder by the machines of modern foresters for the planting of softwoods. When the first crop was taken, the Highland weather would soon wash away the peat and leave another Glen of Weeping, this time for the lost glories of Caledonia.

Storms brewed up in the north-west began to hurl chunks of ice at us as we crossed the high ground. Wildlife was scanty. We saw golden plover and heard the crowing of a grouse. Loch Lomond could be seen gleaming in the vapoury distance.

It was time we took in a little folklore—such as Rob Roy's Cottage at Inverlochlarig, to reach which we would traverse the glen extending just west of Ben More. We felt like pioneers as we plodded through an area not yet popular enough to have a strip of brown mush called a footpath. Higher up, the snow was thawing, as evidenced by flattened vegetation around the white patches and by the general sodden nature of the ground where the drying winds of spring had not yet done their work. As we crossed from one glen to another we met a variety of bogs—quaking bogs, rippling bogs, sucking bogs and those that merely filled our boots with brown water.

The glen beyond was equally desolate. Here was an expanse of the now familiar tussocky vegetation and a landscape complete with boulders, some as big as modern bungalows. We were at least going downhill and made rapid progress. Into view came the Promised Land—Inverlochlarig. The floor of the glen had a hedge-to-hedge carpet of succulent grass. Farms were well-maintained, the stock including ponies, prize sheep and geese. Doubtless, there was milk and honey!

A farm girl pointed out a modern-looking house and said it was where our hero Rob Roy had died. Lunch on a hillock overlooking this house was followed by a slog back up the glen. As we reached the car, the Fredometer noted 13.1 miles.

5 LOOKING FOR NESSIE
The Caledonian Canal

It was a rain-washed morning, with sunlight on the bens and the stub-ends of rainbows gleaming against banks of vapour. A few tatters of cloud wandered among the hills as though looking for an exit. Operation Nessie began when Ian, whose usual job was with the ferryboat on the Isle of Rum, deftly reversed our pleasure craft from the moorings at Inverness into the river and pointed her fiberglass bows towards Banavie Locks, at the southern end of the Caledonian Canal.

When Fred had reported he had 'policeman's heel' we had decided to take the pressure off it by organising a trip down the Canal. George had flown off to Saudi Arabia and John was in an intensive care unit, to which he had been taken when he felt some pains in chest and arms while mowing the lawn at home. Ian was available, to our relief. We appointed him skipper in a ceremony involving 'wee drammies. We were delighted when John reported that he was out of hospital. He had asked the doctor if it was wise for him to go on a cruise: the doctor said the rest and change would do him good. There had been no mention of the Caledonian Canal.

On the 300-mile dash northwards to the Great Glen, we stopped once, for a snack, in a hotel bar that resembled an ancient vault, an effect achieved by chicken wire covered with plaster. At a supermarket in Inverness we filled a trolley with tins and packets of food; the merchandise cost £29 and the weight of it buckled the trolley.

We arrived at the landings to collect our boat as an identical craft returned to base, in a somewhat untidy condition, with a slight list to starboard. The skipper told us about aggressive trawlers at Fort Augustus and five-foot waves on Loch Ness. John, who did not go anywhere without his fishing rod, listened enviously to the tale of the man who had hooked a couple of salmon and given them away to a hotel, not realising that salmon was being sold at £3.50 a pound.

As an expectant grandfather, I rang up home for news. A baby boy had been born to my daughter. Fred proposed we should have a celebratory ceilidh but insisted on being regarded as Senior Grandpa. I was persuaded to drink some whisky. Ian sang a Scottish air and from a lady in the next boat came a rather sad Italian song. Two days' whisky supply was downed by my shipmates in a couple of hours.

Next morning, Fred was suffering from what he called 'alcoholic remorse', and John was thinking of returning to his intensive care unit. I nursed a thick head. Not having been anaesthetised by spirits, I had heard every nocturnal noise, especially the slap of wavelets against the fibre-glass hull and the snoring of a sozzled sleeper.

A booklet gave us the basic facts about the Canal—that it was built between 1803 and 1822, being Britain's first ship-carrying canal and still the only one capable of accommodating ships of up to 500 tons from one side of Britain to the other. The Canal is 60 miles long, of which 22 miles lie in man-made cuttings and 38 miles are through natural lochs.

We proceeded up the Ness river, with Ian on the 'bridge'. He was amused by the simplicity of the charts provided. Loch Ness had a drawing of the Monster and a note recording 900 feet of water. Funnelled by the hills, a westerly wind smothered the top of each wave with spray. For 24 miles we had no real shelter and our boat slammed through the wild water at 3,400 revs, when the recommended cruising speed was 2,000. Pointing to Urquhart Castle, Fred helpfully remarked, 'If you forget the name, just think of Lancashire for "haircut".'

Loch Ness is for fair-weather cruising; it holds the greatest volume of fresh water in Britain and in wild weather it may be as spirited as the open sea. Even the local waterfalls can drench visitors, as happened to Professor Wilson, visiting the Falls of Foyers. He wrote: 'We are drenched as if leaning in a hurricane over the gunwale of a ship, rolling... through a heavy sea. The very solid globe of earth quakes... Has some hill-loch burst its barrier? For what a world of waters comes now tumbling into the abyss! Niagara! hast thou a fiercer roar?'

The Boat Manual had a paragraph about Nessie. A bite from the Monster means almost certain infection with some unknown bacteria; this results in a dangerous illness that is only treatable by placing six-week-old kippers on the wound, twice daily, for four days! John smiled when it was suggested that he might catch the Monster with his rod and line, which had been in use over the stern since we left the river. He went below for a 'wee dram'. We swung into action, drawing in the line, replacing the bait with a plastic model of the Monster and casting again. John returned to the deck. He swung into action when he saw he had at last caught a fish. The reel hummed, the line shortened and the catch bobbed along the surface. For a second or two, he was unsure what he had caught. Then his face crinkled into a broad smile.

This being Saturday evening, we were anxious to negotiate the flight of locks at Fort Augustus before they were closed, for nothing would persuade the Canal authority to open them on a Sunday. We found ourselves in the Kytra stretch with no competition. John, while trolling from the boat, caught a trout (which he would cook in breadcrumbs for breakfast). Our craft was lightly moored near a lock.

We had not reckoned with the peculiar currents of the Canal. I awoke to the periodical bumping of the craft against the masonry as water welled up in the vicinity of the lock gates, and as I listened I became aware of other sounds—the pattering of rain and rasp-like snoring.

In brightening conditions on the Sunday afternoon, I climbed the nearest hill looking for deer. Five sika stags were disturbed near a small plantation; they went off bouncingly, as though their legs were fitted with springs, and as their excitement mounted they showed more of the white caudal discs. One of the deer called—a high-pitched squeal that sounded from a distance like a clear whistle, the pipe of a Northern Pan. Of the eleven red stags I saw, four had cast their antlers. I fraternised with two garrons (the type of pony used to carry the bodies of slain deer off the hill) and descended through a birch wood where primroses were beginning to bloom.

Moving off next morning, we came to Cullochy Lock and found it to be manned by a Lancashireman. He had been made redundant and told his wife he would go to Scotland and stay there until he had another job and a house. She did not have to wait for long before being invited to join him in the Highlands.

We bought provisions at the shop, then voyaged on to Loch Oich, where the sight of sand martins taking insects low over the water stimulated John to get out his fishing tackle. We discovered the fridge had 'gone out' and so we jettisoned half a gallon of white liquid that had been ice-cream. The effect on the water was that of a giant gull dropping that soon dispersed and disappeared.

For the final stretch, John and I walked on the towpath. The Canal meandered between high banks, with views of the big bens and the river. Buzzards circled and mewed. The surroundings must have impressed those Scottish deep-sea fishermen who, prior to the making of the Canal, had faced stormy conditions when sailing through the Pentland Firth. The Canal schemes of the eighteenth century came to nought. Early last century, security was in the minds of those who drew up the Act, for British shipping was vulnerable to attack by French privateers.

The story of this engineering achievement has often been told. John and I discussed the human aspects—the tendency of the labourers to sip whisky and the efforts to encourage them to take ale instead; also the capricious nature of the labour force when there were pressing jobs elsewhere, such as fishing for herring or lifting potatoes.

We moored the boat near the top of Neptune's Staircase, the name given to the series of eight locks at Banavie. I was the first to venture from the boat early on the following morning. The wind had dropped. Every object was perfectly reflected in the canal.

Fred had an ambition to go by train from Banavie to Mallaig, which according to the timetable was relatively easy. Ben Nevis was the main point of interest from the platform, but after half an hour even this view began to pall. I inquired about the train. 'It's ten minutes late.' A pause, then: 'It usually is.' It had 'broken down' at Spean Bridge and no one seemed surprised when it clattered into the station half an hour late.

The tracks lay beside the sea loch. I saw drake eider looking like two-tone buoys. Then we entered a world of hills and lochans, with the train following an adventurous, ever-winding course through cuttings and tunnels, under bridges, beside birch woods and lochans where the cigar-like forms of red-throated divers were to be seen. Now and again, a red stag broke the skyline. 'Cement Billy' (Macalpine) had jubilantly trundled his cement-mixer to the course of the line and turned out the great viaduct at Glenfinnan and many a lesser bridge in gleaming concrete. The train stopped here and there but our inclination was to look westwards, for a first glimpse of two of the Small Isles, Eigg and Rum, now just smudges of grey, for the weather had closed in with mist and rain.

At Mallaig, there was time to dine at the Fisherman's Mission on cottage pie and chips. We inquired about the old *Loch Arkaig*, to be told that she had sunk in the harbour and been towed to the Clyde. Doing duty until another ferry became available was the *Coll*, which reminded me of a tank landing craft. Mallaig was its usual noisy self, alive with gulls. We watched the arrival of the first of 60 trawlers that had been operating in the Minch at from 90 to 120 fathoms.

Back at the boat, Ian had prepared a delectable meal, including chicken. We sat and chatted until, with the bottoming of a bottle of whisky, a visitor left and we had eight miles to travel on a darkening canal. The water was flat calm, which was confusing. We could not always be sure just where the land ended and the water began. Trout were rising. Startled duck were diving. It was dusk when we reached the locks.

Our boat was cleverly manoeuvred until it was floating side-on towards a moored cabin cruiser. We watched, fascinated, as the moored boat came closer. The curtains had not been closed. There were lights within the cabin: a party was in progress; We brushed against the boat. After a moment of shocked silence, the curtains were drawn and some music switched off. We did not hear another sound and, next morning, we moved off before those in the other boat had bestirred themselves...

At Kytra lock, by far the most picturesque in my opinion, we tied up to allow a trawler bound for Fraserburgh to enter first. The weather was so good a general benevolence could be detected. I saw the hard northern light picking out fine details of the bottle-green of Scots pines.

We proceeded up the canal, dressed overall in wet towels. As we moored near the upper lock at Fort Augustus, a lad with the unmistakable twang of North East England rushed up and exclaimed: 'Eh, mister. That bwoat over there has only hawf a propeller. He's hit the fishing bwoat!' This did not cause the fishermen a moment's worry.

One of them handed me a huge, not very attractive sea fish. We photographed John holding it in one hand, with his fishing tackle in the other, and then handed the fish to a stroller on the towpath. He thanked us, then looked at our boat, sniffed and said 'I used to work for a boat-builder. He used fibre-glass. My boss gave me what looked like a large bath and told me to fit it out!'

Next morning, we were among the first to begin the half-hour descent of Fort Augustus's impressive series of locks. The fishing craft surged ahead, travelling fast, emitting a thick fug of diesel fumes. A considerable wash hit a row of moored boats, causing them to dance at the end of their mooring ropes. We later chatted with a young man who had been hurled from his bunk.

We had returned to Loch Ness and, with time to spare, entered Urquhart Bay to allow John to troll for fish (none was caught.) A swan paddled half a mile to join us and was rewarded with a slice of bread. No Monster appeared. Where the loch began to give way to the river at the swing bridge, a hitherto placid watercourse was being churned up by boats into an oceanic chaos of waves and spume. John caught a fish! At least, he hooked one. The reel sang as the line ran out, but he had no chance to play the fish and soon the line parted.

We reached the mooring at 5.20 p.m. The laddie at the fuel pump told us we had used 30 gallons of diesel. The average consumption is 27 gallons. As good Yorkshiremen, not inclined to throw 'brass' about, we tried in vain to account for those extra three gallons.

6 THE ROAD TO THE ISLES
Fort William to Mallaig

We journeyed northwards from Yorkshire for 390 miles, passing through a tropical zone to Perth, where scores of grey geese were tattie-howking on new-ploughed land. At Perth, George's wife provided us with a nourishing meal and we resumed our northward progress, passing a food-house called The Frying Scotsman.

Most of the red deer were on parade in the Drumochter area, with several hundred stags grazing on high ground. Parties of hinds were in the peaty hollows near the railway. Easter was early that year. Near Dalwhinnie, the first of the tourist coaches emerged from a blizzard. The sky cleared as we motored by Loch Laggan. More red deer were recorded.

From Fort William, we followed the Road to the Isles, passing a hostelry offering 'Bed and English Breakfast'. At Lochailort, the hotel we selected had a photograph of a Highland loch surrounded by tall hills. It was captioned: 'The source of your bathwater'. Fred shuddered. He then looked around, shivered and remarked, 'It's a right West Highland situation—all the windows are open.' At a local pub, to which we resorted for a short time, young people were listening to noisy music and investing their social security payments in liquid assets. We left, standing for a time in the warm, still air, with pipistrelle bats making patterns around us.

The famous song 'The Road to the Isles' related to an old droving route. It was really the Road from the Isles for the hundreds of cattle reared on Skye, which were coaxed into the narrows between Kylerhea and Bernera, near Glenelg, and swam across, to be driven along one of several routes leading to the autumn trysts at Crieff and later Falkirk, where they were bought by the lowland graziers. One route lay beside Loch Hourn; I tramped part of it and met a man living in an amphibious vehicle, who was intending to make a film about the droving days.

The Road to the Isles of popular appeal is the A.830 to Mallaig, but the road-makers, while improving its line and surface, robbed it of some of its romance. Nonetheless, my favourite Highland view is along this road: the place between Arisaig and Mallaig where the road dips near the sea and one looks across silver sands and machair to the blue-green sea on which the islands—Eigg, Rum and Skye—appear to be floating.

At one of the hotels on the Road to the Isles, I inquired about breakfast-time, to he told: 'Listen for the pipes.' Was the plumbing unduly noisy as people bestirred themselves in the early morning? At 8.15, as I descended the grand staircase in what had once been a big hoose, the centerpiece of a sporting estate, the pipes sounded with a vengeance as the owner, in full Highland dress, marched up and down the hall with the pipes in full cry.

It did not take us long to settle into the languid West Highland routine. No one seemed to know it was Easter; People were still going late to their beds (around 1.30) and were correspondingly late to rise. We awoke to wind and rain. George announced we would be seeking Glen Mama. We crossed the railway track, admiring a profusion of wood anemones by the trees and an acre or two of bog myrtle, which George called 'Poor Man's Lavender'. He invited me to break off some leaves; these were crushed between our fingers. We sniffed. The aroma was indeed akin to that of lavender.

The hills were alive with red deer. Three hinds grazed the sheltered side of a knoll not far from the inn. We disturbed a dozen uncast red stags. The grizzle-grey winter coats toned with the bent-grasses and banks of old heather. A party of 36 grey geese, in two chevrons, passed below the level of the highest bens. Our little party breasted the ridge and looked down into long, dark Loch Mama. Immense crags gave character to the flanking hills, and George diagnosed peregrine country.

Our descent was through an ancient birch wood. Deer and sheep had prevented the natural regeneration of timber, so the remaining birch trees were old. They had taken root among boulders which in the damp conditions had grown cushions of moss. The branches of the trees were draped with moss and bracket fungus adorned the black and silver trunks. Elsewhere, trees that had fallen were sprouting holly and rowan, the seeds having presumably lodged in the spongy mass of dead wood. I found myself humming strains from Grieg.

In the glen, cattle were waiting for their calves to be born. We walked beside the remains of blackhouses and lazybeds. Red deer hinds were grazing the flats beside an inflowing burn.

That evening, the lads were soon among the 'wee drammies'. It was a relief to learn that the traditional food of the Highlands was no longer salt herring and tatties. Fred expanded on his theory that the Highland Line is not a geological concept at all but the division between two food zones—things served with chips (south) and things served with boiled potatoes (north). George said that in this part of the world it was necessary to answer a question with a question. We later asked: 'How're your feet?' He replied: 'Which feet?'

At 11 p.m., Ron went to the car and returned with the news that it was snowing. The local red deer stags had been visiting the hotel dustbins.

Next morning, the only snow was that lying in patches in the ancient joints of the hills. We planned to seek one of the Prince Charlie Caves. Striding out briskly, we crossed Alt na Criche at about 1,000 feet and entered a 'lost' glen near Loch Beorald. We covered rather more than 12 hard miles and were on our feet for eight hours.

We entered a wet wilderness, with not a blade of green vegetation and 'nowt stirring', except the hearts, legs and cigarettes of our adventurers; we followed a line of telegraph poles that looked grey and careworn, like a row of dead birches. We contended with the usual succession of 'false summits'—which Ron said was 'summit and nowt'—and negotiated a few bogs before we stood on some rocks and beheld Loch Beorald, about three miles long; with a Wastwaterish (Lakeland) setting of upsweeping ground.

Prince Charlie's Cave, said to contain a bottle of whisky, was not easy to locate. There were scores of caves. George told the romantic story of Charlie's landing from French frigates and of his dash over the hill to escape the redcoats. Ron, with astonishing patience and superb map-reading, located the cave. Fred emerged with some empty beer cans. 'If Whitehall knew about the squalid and insanitary conditions, he'd have been left to his fate,' he said.

We traversed the glen, to the shores of Morar, where—as George observed—'the grass is green, not yellow or orange'. Our line of telegraph poles was joined by a row of poles carrying electricity from the owner's own hydroelectric scheme. Some posts had been battered by red stags, which in their frenzy at the time of the rut had puddled up the peat round about.

We listened to the clicks and whistles of a cock wheatear, which had no difficulty in reaching this hidden glen, Meoble, whereas we had slogged our way over the top and most visitors arrived by boat or helicopter. It was a well-cared-for place, but we saw traces of what had been—a blackhouse now roofed with corrugated iron and presumably used as a storage place; also a school house in corrugated iron, with corrugated iron forming the toilet building which had been used the day before yesterday, for the school was now closed.

A Highland bull lumbered across sodden grassland. A boat from the glen was now heading down Loch Morar in such choppy conditions that spray was breaking over the wheelhouse. The local graveyard, bright with daffodils; was full of anonymous people, for the wind and frost had scoured the inscriptions from the tombstones.

Our way out of the glen was along an old cattle-track running diagonally from a bridge spanning a foaming burn. We heard later that when cattle were driven this way in 1981, they 'broke back' and—such was the difficulty of regrouping them—were left in the glen, with the hope that they could be persuaded to leave next time.

Slop, slop, over peat and sphagnum moss, by burn and bog, wet stone, glowing lichen, succulent moss—we plodded up a typical Scottish glenside, passing the remains of a building that was small, crude of construction, possibly the summertime lodging of those who cared for the cattle and sheep on the upper slopes during the short Highland summer.

We broke the skyline and began the long descent to Lochailort in a wee shower which became something akin to a cloudburst. Fred reported water pouring from the eyelet-holes of his boots. We handed our wet clothes to the good ladies in the kitchen of the hotel. Ron crooned 'The Road to the Isles', including among the lochs seen a new stretch of water—Loch Aga.

We made inquiries about hiring a boat for a trip to a remote peninsula.

'Where would he drop us off?' asked George.

'Och,' said the local man who had agreed to make the arrangements, 'if I told you the Gaelic name, it would mean nothing to you!'

It was a chilly but bright dawn, with a powder-blue sky. We chatted about the Highlander's partiality for whisky and about the famous 'early surgery' that led him to visit a hostelry as soon as mine host could be persuaded to open a bottle. Ron recalled a customer he had overheard at breakfast-time in Braemar: he asked for 'a large dram and a wee whale (kipper)'.

By mid-morning, we were in a lobster boat heading for a beach of silver sand near the point of Ardnish, an area now deserted by humans who had formerly lived off the land (tatties) and the sea (fish). We passed some of the islets of Loch nan Uamh, which were festooned by herring gulls and greater black-backed gulls, with a few pairs of oystercatchers. Where the water became bumpy, we were told there was 'nothing between us and America'. Nobody cheered.

A raven flew over, but we had little time to debate whether it was a good or bad omen. The black guillemot that cruised by was still in its whitish winter plumage. We rounded the point into calmer water, scattering shags from their nesting islets. We disembarked from the boat by leaping from the bows onto the sand—between waves.

Many of the houses in the 'lost' settlement on Ardnish were lined up with a raised beach of rock and shell-sand. Behind them stretched an area that generations of residents had patiently cultivated as 'lazybeds' but which was now neglected and full of 'rush bobs'. Fred remarked: 'In a place like this, they'd be beggered if they didn't fish.' Later, he said, 'Just fancy—a man feels hungry; his stomach's rumbling. Somebody gives him a bow and arrow and says: "Go and get a deer!"'

Our exit from Ardnish was by a paved path stretching three miles to the root of the peninsula and the hard road just west of Lochailort. A durable surface was provided by slabs of gabbro, with ditching on either side where this was possible.

Trudging along the Ardnish equivalent of the M.1 was a delight.

It began with a climb through birchwoods, in the company of buzzards. We passed mossy stones, the mossiness indicating not only a high rainfall but clean air. Where the route broke out of tree cover onto the open hill, we saw the sun bring a gleam to the black plumage of ravens. At the highest point we could look westwards to the isles of Eigg and Rum, set in a turquoise sea.

Back at the hotel, a local man was entertaining the company with his tales of a man who had been so drunk that if he had opened his eyes he would have bled to death. The local's dog began to bark, and it was not commanded to be quiet. 'Och,' said the owner, 'it's only barking at a tourist!'

Another day, at a country inn south of Loch Ailort, we heard of the Highlander who announced a wine and cormorant-tasting party. 'Naebody turned up.' The conversation continued to be related to food. We were told that a cormorant was once a food item in the Highlands. 'When I shot one, I buried it for three weeks. I then dug up the bird, skinned it and soaked the flesh for three days, then boiled it for a further three days... I fried it and served it with a saw.' Cormorants and shags caught in the Hebrides had their oil glands promptly removed, were skinned and sent to London, to be sold as Hebridean Chickens, until someone discovered their true identity. The market slumped.

On the following day, we were in the area between Morar and Nevis, right on the edge of a cloud mass. To the west was clear sky and blue water; to the east, the big bens were wrapped in cloud.

We had scarcely set foot on the hill when the sound of geese reached us. They were the cries of greylags. Now that the northerly wind had slackened, the geese were impelled to fly northwards to their nesting grounds in Iceland, some 500 miles away. About 60 geese flew just above the rim of the hills beyond Morar; a second skein, of some 20 birds, was half a mile behind.

We observed leadership changes in the main group as the birds crossed the Sound of Sleat; the two groups merged and, viewed distantly, looked like dark beads strung across the sky.

We walked from Bracorina to Stoule, across the moors, passing a lochan on which floated a goldeneye drake. Meadow pipits were displaying over the heather. We descended to yet another 'lost' village, though the main farmhouse was being used, perhaps by a shepherd.

On our return across the tops by a different route, we surprised a young stag—and then surprised ourselves! For some reason, we left the main path to walk a ridge. At the end of the ridge, we quested for the path. Walking became mountaineering. Under the gaze of startled ravens, we descended 1,000 feet in about 20 minutes by crag-hopping, slithering on scree, bounding from tuft to tuft of coarse grass and clambering over boulders.

By the time the ravens had settled down, we were at the loch, overlooking a black-throated diver. Near the car, we watched a small girl feeding banana skins to some Hereford cattle.

When I awoke next morning, I briskly rubbed one leg with the other—and realised that the itching came from a sheep tick, the dreaded Black Spot o' the Heilands. It must have climbed aboard when we had a snack meal on the hill above Morar. The mite would become a monstrous object, like a black grape, as it gorged itself on blood: my blood! George, our witch-doctor, advised 'spirits', but I could never recall whisky being useful. The doctor at home later smiled when I mentioned it and asked, 'Did you want to drown the tick?' George mentioned turpentine. I shook my head. 'Och, then, here's some Dettol.'

I shuddered when another day on the hill was proposed. Perhaps I could eat and have a mid-day nap while standing up and thereby cheat the ticks. We motored by Eilt and watched red-throated divers admiring their reflections on the mirror of a calm loch. We parked the car at Glenfinnan and walked under Concrete Billy Macalpine's famous railway viaduct. A pair of goosander passed, having flown under one of the arches.

We were overtaken by a Munro-basher, a young man who disappeared from our view in a cloud of cigarette smoke. Perhaps he expected to encounter ticks or midges.

A red stag broke the skyline; a dozen hinds appeared from birch cover and grazed the upper slopes. George pointed excitedly at Stob Coire nan Ceare, a splendid high summit, close on 3,000 feet above sea level. Cruising around the hill's craggy top was a golden eagle, which eventually moved off towards the Streap, partly gliding, partly flapping in the listless air.

We dined (ate a few sandwiches and some fruit) where the burn was sunk between rocks. A rowan tree gave an artistic touch to the scene.

George announced that we would cross the ridge and return to the car by way of Glen Lighe. 'There are two ways of tackling the ridge. We can go farther up the glen and contour back, or'—and one could tell by the look on his face that he had already made up his mind—'there's Sudden Death.' By this he meant the to-hell-with-it approach, straight up the slope. This was the way we went, from the glen bottom to the alpine zone without deviation. The air chilled, the vegetation became more sparse and coarse, a few patches of snow were passed and soon the upper burn was seen to be crusty with ice.

Pausing for the umpteenth time, I watched a large herd of red deer grazing near snow, just below a line of cliffs that were only a shade or two deeper than the tatters of cloud. We entered the region of plants with long roots and short stems.

Any standing water was iced over, and the snow squeaked under foot.

We rounded some rocks and beheld a skyline worthy of the Alps. Below us was Glen Lighe, soggy with peat and almost devoid of trees. A burn took the longest possible course down the, valley, with many an ox-bow. Beyond, the ground swept upwards to a grassy ridge, so smooth it was as though the Pleistocene ice had just melted from it. Beyond were other ridges, and the highest places were patched with snow.

Between them and a sky that held broad bands of tone, like hastily applied water-colours, were snow-capped peaks. Ben Nevis was the centrepiece. Something akin to an alpen glow gave them a romantic touch. A ptarmigan, the alpine grouse, gave a frog-like croaking as it departed from almost under our feet, leaving the hill to ourselves—and the deer.

7 OVER THE SEA TO RUM
The Small Isles

We rose at 4.30 a.m., giving ourselves plenty of time to catch the boat at Mallaig. We shut the front door of the hotel, hearing the click of the Yale lock, and clambered into the car to be driven furiously along the winding road through Arisaig to Mallaig. The headlamp beam revealed a red stag grazing about ten yards from the road.

At Mallaig, the *Pioneer* (1,000 tons) moved restlessly at her moorings. She was being used for three weeks on the Small Isles run while the regular vessel had an overhaul. A herring gull called, proclaiming a new day. The deck lights of the *Pioneer* revealed slanting rain. We left promptly at 6 a.m., and soon Mallaig was a blur. The big boat began to pitch and slam in a corrugated, foam-flecked sea.

I have had some uneasy nights at Mallaig. There was the time when, with members of the British Deer Society, I had to share a bed with a Scotsman who had drunk whisky until well into the night—and then flopped, into a drunken stupor and snored so hard the bedroom window rattled. As if that was not enough, a ceilidh was in progress in a wooden hut across the way· and turning-out time was marked with much shouting, singing and car door slamming.

Mallaig nights were never long. On bed and breakfast occasions, there would be a kick on the door of our selected quarters in good time for us to stagger out of bed and dress to catch the boat, which left long before daybreak and often—

this being early springtime—with flurries of snow showing in the light of the deck lamps.

On my first crossing to Rum, in *The Western Isles*, skippered by Brucie Watts, of Mallaig, the sea was lively and the boat on a tilt, so that when I reached the other side my legs ached from maintaining an unnatural position on deck. Later I came to know the *Loch Arkaig*, a wooden-hulled vessel with a load of iron as ballast, which wallowed in the sea like a surfacing whale. On my first trip in her I marvelled that there was no hold for goods and no covered space for cattle or sheep; the solitary beast, a bull bound for Eigg, was hauled aboard in a special box which prevented the animal from moving far. A passenger on that voyage mentioned the old days and sighed for the lost glories—when *Lochmor* served the Small Isles, offering lounge, dining room and cabins, as well as good accommodation for 35 head of cattle and some 120 lambs, the products of the Isles.

Willie Callander was our favourite skipper. He would invite us, one at a time, into his diminutive cabin, there to discuss Gaelic prose and song. He had a notion that gulls were the reincarnation of old seamen, some having stripes on their wings. (He was doubtless thinking of the brown marks on immature birds.) When Willie retired, we presented him with a bird book, which pleased him immensely.

Fred and I chatted with a young couple who seemed more suited to city streets than the Hebrides. The girl wore fashionable clothes and had a modern hair style. She told us that her father worked on Canna. Fred asked what he did on the island. The girl looked to where waves were breaking on naked rock and treeless hills, and replied, 'God knows!'

The *Pioneer* inched its way to the jetty on Canna—the only jetty on the Small Isles—under the expert gaze of a Scottish terrier we had seen before. The propellers stirred the sea into a milky white. I watched a black guillemot dive, showing off its red legs, its exhaled air presumably adding to the seething mass of bubbles.

Fred and I had been the first of our little group to visit Canna, some years before, and now the memories came flooding back. We had booked for several days a bothy tenanted by Mary Anne, who lived at another house on the shore. A gracious old lady, soft-spoken and with all the Gaelic charm, she served tea in fine china and we each received a piece of Lyon's swiss roll, fresh off the boat.

We walked to the bothy along a track that had been submerged, this being high water, so that a diversion had to be made across a marshy field. The bothy was a substantial detached house standing not far from the footbridge connecting Canna to its satellite island, Sanday. Two bedrooms were far enough apart for the sleepers to be out of snoring range of each other. From the taps in the bathroom came water tinted like whisky.

We had the use of a Rayburn stove in the living room, the fuel being driftwood from the beach and coal brought in by 'puffer' from the Clyde. Fred established himself in the kitchen and soon put together a meal—steak and kidney pies, somewhat squashed after the sea journey; dehydrated potato; tinned beans, sliced bread and soft margarine.

Then I walked to the village to telephone. The metalwork on the kiosk was painted blue and the door was hanging off, having been vandalised by the weather. I recall with delight that the *burr, burr* of the dialling tone merged with the crooning of eider drakes on the rising tide.

That first trip was enlivened by a party of Scottish schoolboys, with their teachers, who were on a bird-watching holiday— complete with torches for dazzling shearwaters, hooks for grabbing nesting shags, a taped recording of a male corncrake, to be used for enticing a local bird into a mist-net, and a hammer which would be ideal for knocking teeth from the corpse of a beached shark.

'Would you like to go shearwatering?' asked a freckle-faced lad. We nodded. He said the party was setting off at 11 p.m. It was almost dark but warm, with no perceptible movement of air or sea, as we walked towards the northern end of Canna and then scrambled up a slope that we would not have dreamed of tackling in daylight. We then sat waiting for conditions to suit the Manx shearwaters.

These seabirds lay their eggs in burrows. The changeover in incubation duties occurs in the dark of night, when the main predators, big gulls, are roosting. The summer night is short and much has to be packed into a few hours. Shearwaters arrive with rustling wings and circle with yodelling calls before pitching down near their burrows. How each bird locates its own burrow among so many in such confusing circumstances I do not know, unless there is a distinctive scent or a finely-tuned sense of direction.

The schoolboys intended to grasp homecoming shearwaters after dazzling them with a torch. Numbered rings would be attached to their legs so that a check might be kept on their movements. It was not a good night for shearwatering and the loom of a lighthouse on a rock stack far to the west ensured it would never be completely dark. I heard the croak of a bird in flight. The flanking cliffs created an echo-chamber in which the sound took on a special quality.

The lad to my immediate right gave a cry of joy as a bird landed with a thump near him; he shone the torch in its face and grabbed the hapless shearwater. I saw a pigeon-sized bird, dark above, with wings of considerable length. Several bird-watchers mustered; the alloy ring was placed over one leg-and the shearwater left to recover its wits and composure. We returned home in the wee small hours. The rasping voice of the local corncrake kept all and sundry awake.

The same freckle-faced boy turned up at the bothy on the following evening and invited us to go 'craking'. At 10 p.m., with the weather cooler than of late, we repaired with four budding ornithologists to a meadow where they set up a tape-recorder and, before it, a mist net. The tape-recorder was switched on and the double-barrelled call of a corncrake (recorded on another island) could now be heard. Hopefully, the local bird, not recognising the rival cock, would fly to investigate and become entangled in the mist net. That was the theory and up to a point it was successful that night. The local corncrake flew in, but when it was just short of the net it landed and walked away! At 10.30 p.m., when there was nothing more to report, the net was packed away.

We were awakened next day by the crooning of eiders on the high tide. We breakfasted on grapefruit juice followed by bacon and eggs, and sat in the sun, watching terns darting about the sky, the birds' gracefulness offset by their coarse voices.

That day, on the heights of Canna, in an atmosphere of considerable clarity, we saw the Outer Hebrides as a line of blue hummocks which, at the nearest point, were over 30 miles away. The Cuillins of Skye looked so close, at 20 miles, we felt we could have tossed a bonnet over one of them. We returned to the longer views—to a sighting of Neise Point lighthouse at 30–35 miles and what must surely be Harris at 60 miles.

I envied the white-tailed sea eagle its extra visibility as it soared on such a day. We did not see an eagle but we knew from a meeting with John Love, who supervised the introductory scheme on Rum, that sea eagles had settled on Canna. Among the tangle of old heather and the orchids that grew in profusion, lay a flight feather of an immature eagle. Eventually, we stood near the rim of a range of cliffs over 600 feet high, while a peregrine falcon rose with the wind. Far down, between the clifftop and the sea, was a grassy slope, a highly suitable place for puffins.

The fence along the cliffs was to restrict goats to the cliff faces and to keep sheep off them. We heard of shags nesting on the northern coast—86 were hooked and ringed by the young ornithologists—and of grey seals pupping near Garrisdale.

Fred and I had an hour to spare at the end of our visit to Canna. We might have wandered down to the modest jetty to watch the eiders and black guillemots, and to look eastwards for a first glimpse of the ferry from Mallaig. We might have stared at cliffs plastered with multicoloured graffiti. The first large drops of rain heralding a storm sent us scuttering into the Church of Scotland. We used the premises as both a sanctuary and an umbrella. We had admired this venerable-looking building, with its round tower, Irish style, and had several times studied a wrought iron gate with its pictorial representations of local features.

When the Welshman, Pennant, visited Canna towards the end of the eighteenth century, he discovered that both the minister and the 'popist Priest' of Canna lived on Eigg.

I admire the moderation of their congregation who attend the preaching of either indifferently as they happen to arrive. As the Scotch are economists in religion, I would recommend to them the practice of one of the little Swiss mixed cantons who, through mere frugality, kept but one divine; a moderate honest fellow who, steering clear of controversial points, held forth to the Calvinist flock on one part of the day, and to his Catholic on the other. He lived long among them much respected, and died lamented.

Fred believed that, in the absence of resident ministers, the two churches must co-operate today. We had seen the imposing Catholic Church but had not heard of a resident priest. We knew—because we had stayed with him—that the Church of Scotland missionary for the Small Isles had his manse and principal church on Eigg. He hoped to attend at least one service on Canna a year. What happened to the money placed on the collection plate by weekday visitors? Fred made inquiries—and discovered that a Catholic periodically emptied the plate and, on a shopping trip by boat to Mallaig, put the money in a Church of Scotland account at the Bank!

Now, half-a-dozen years later, as the *Pioneer* cruised in calm waters at the lee of Rum, the much-heralded 'window' in the weather system appeared. Passengers began to cast their outer garments. We sailed within easy viewing range of Bloodstone Hill, with its flat pate and awesome sea cliff, where the semi-precious stone, bloodstone, was once obtained.

Wild waves were breaking on the sandy beach at Kilmory, where Fiona Guinness and students conduct long-term research into the biology of red deer. Through binoculars, I picked out her cottage, which had been a ruin when first she moved here; I also saw the old laundry of the Bullough family, the former owners of Rum.

We rounded the point to enter Loch Scresort, seeing the Torridonian terraces—sandstones and shales in conspicuous beds, shifted a little from the horizontal by some ancient land disturbance, so that one had the impression that the landscape was slipping beneath the sea. We saw the peaks of Rum, like gigantic bell tents, to the south of the loch.

The *Pioneer* could not venture far into Loch Scresort, but the island boat *Rhouma*, with our old friend Ian in charge, awaited us. Within minutes, passengers and goods had been switched from one craft to the other, and we were riding the waves towards Kinloch, where the rose-red castle built by the Bulloughs rose in majesty above trees—a rare sight on this wild, storm-lashed Hebridean island.

Rum has the shape of a diamond, each axis measuring eight miles; but that is where comparison with a diamond must end, for I have never seen Rum sparkle. Rather it is a dour island, wearing dull tones—a barren island, indeed.

The highest hill, Sgurr nan Gillean, has its base at sea level and its head at an elevation of 2,503 feet. The walker reaches the summit in less than one mile. Sgurr nan Gillean is a Gaelic name on an island where Norse words form the language of topography—Barkeval and Hallival, Askival and Trollaval, Ainshval and Ruinsival.

Rum is a great weather factory. Its cuillins manufacture cloud and the precipitation is like a torrent from a celestial hosepipe. I have awakened at Kinloch to hear the rain falling with the intensity of a tropical monsoon, the pitch of sound scarcely altering from one hour to another. Fred and Ron had a true Highland baptism when they first visited Rum. The crossing from Mallaig was wet and windy; the rain scarcely eased during the time they were on the island, and on a major walk they were swaddled in waterproof clothing, fighting off clouds of insects that were desperate to bite them.

My own introduction was in somewhat better conditions; I climbed the Torridonian terraces north of Loch Scresort and beheld Kinloch Castle among its imported trees far below. I saw the great hills on their base of Lewisian gneiss and, south-eastwards, the long smooth shape of Eigg.

When the sun shines, and the mountain-top clouds are white rather than dark grey, Rum is enchanting. There may be russet tones on the landscape until well into spring, but moderating conditions do bring a flush of fresh green to the wee glens radiating from the island's centre, and especially to the flats by the beach where the red deer graze in the old crofting areas, the deer offering their hard round pellets of waste material to the god of fertility.

Anyone who thinks of the Hebridean life as changeless might ponder on the isle of Rum, which has had long periods of unsettlement. The name of the island has itself changed several times. The Norsefolk, impressed by its spaciousness, called it Rom. In due course, it became Ruma, then Rum. In recent years the spelling 'Rhum' has become general, although it is frowned on by purists.

Little trace of Norse occupation has been discovered, but Rum did once prove to be a benevolent island; by the late 1700s some 440 people lived on the tracts of better land. Whenever we go to Rum, we walk beside the southern shore of Loch Scresort and on to the Deserted Village—deserted by all but gulls and wheatears. At Harris, red deer now graze on the old crofting land. The owner in 1828, wanting to follow the latest craze in the Highlands and, introduce sheep, shipped the people of Rum to North America and brought in a few shepherds and 8,000 sheep. In the days of John Bullough, the sheep yielded to the red deer. Rum became the property of the Nature Conservancy in 1957, and when I first visited the island, a few years later, only the schoolmistress was not an employee of the Conservancy.

Sir George Bullough made the biggest mark on Rum, which he took over from his father in 1891. Father had lived in Kinloch House, built by Dr Maclean, who was tacksman of Rum. Sir George planned Kinloch Castle on the grand scale, and furnished it splendidly in the Edwardian style. The Castle took shape in the first two years of this century. The laird of Rum arranged for heated tanks in which turtles and alligators were kept; he imported a white Arab stallion to improve the stock of the native Rum ponies, which were said to have descended from stock that swam ashore when a galleon of the Spanish Armada grounded on the island. It is a good story, until you are told the ponies came from Eriskay; they were used for work on the farm and to bring down from the hill the bodies of slain stags.

I have wandered through the gardens at Kinloch—in which Bulloughs' gardeners grew the usual run of vegetables, plus exotic fruits like muscatel grapes, figs, peaches and nectarines. The rose and Italian gardens were admired by all who came.

Fourteen gardeners were kept busy. When Sir George and his guests decided to travel across the island, they did so on smooth roads in horse-drawn carriages or sleek Albion cars.

All this opulence—so surprising on a small Hebridean island—lasted for about a dozen years. The outbreak of the 1914–18 war led to the estate being put on a care and maintenance basis, Afterwards, the Bulloughs visited Rum for brief periods only. Sir George died in 1939; his widow sold the island and all upon it to the Nature Conservancy for a nominal sum. It became a study area and, in restricted island conditions, experiments are undertaken of possible value to mainland areas as well.

Fred and I elected to walk to Ian's house, where we had arranged to stay. We strode joyously through woodland which had its fresh spring growth and was soaking up some unaccustomed sunshine. We crossed the bridge spanning the little river, pausing to admire Rum ponies on the hillside. A wee shower swept the area. A 'bright period' turned into a mini-heat wave. It would last for days, during which time the temperature would soar and north-west Scotland would become the hottest part of Europe.

Ian, Kathie and their family lived on Rum, and we arrived at their cottage as though visiting a second home. At the breakfast table, we were provided with knife, fork, spoon and binoculars, for the window framed a view of Loch Scresort, and it was possible that a golden eagle might be beating the bounds of its territory. A corncrake was occasionally seen on the garden path, where it was stalked by the household cat.

We usually had a snack meal on the hill. When we returned to the cottage, we could be assured of a hot stove on which to dry out our sodden clothes and a wee dram to restore a glow to the body; and a good talk with the Simpsons or the opportunity to look at their superb Scottish library until the evening meal, when the main course included venison from the cull of island deer. Before the village was fenced off, deer wandered onto the

The Arran ferry on the Clyde coast.

Glenfinnan viaduct, on the railroad to the Isles.

Thatched home near Bunessan, island of Mull.

George at Prince Charles' Cave, Meoble.

Light refreshments at Glen Eichaig.

... and a mid-day snooze to follow.

The dramatic approach to Glencoe.

Waves beat against the basalt pillars of Staffa.

A puffin, nesting in a burrow above a roaring sea.

Cormorants were once a food item in the islands.

A natural scene on the Caledonian Canal.

Banavie, on the Caledonian Canal.

A misty prospect for Fred on Hanival, Rum.

Highland cattle at Harris, south-west Rum.

George and Fred on the Sgurr of Eigg.

A young Norwegian sea eagle, introduced to Rum.

John tries his angling luck on
Loch Hourn.

Bothy-cleaning day, by Loch Hourn.

Ladhar Bheinn, approached from Loch Hourn.

Kyleakin, on the island of Skye.

A boat by a storm beach on one of the Summer Isles.

Cape Wrath, the Norse "turning point".

A visitor jogs on the village street, St Kilda.

Sign outside an Army refreshment area, St Kilda.

Sunset at Durness, in Sutherland.

Flower-bedecked pastures at Durness.

Handa, a wedge-shaped island ending in lofty cliffs.

Lerwick, on the largest island of the complex Shetland group.

Shetland ram. Such sheep are usually plucked, not clipped.

Muckle Flugga and the Outstack, viewed from Unst.

A fulmar bade us farewell at northermost Scotland.

shore, eating seaweed or grazing by the river. It was nothing unusual to find a cast antler. This would be left for the deer to chew and restore to their system something of the calcium lost in the period of antler growth.

We spent one day crossing the island from east to west—from the beach of shingle and weed, where the hooded crows poked and pried, looking for food, to a beach where the shingle was being stirred by Atlantic rollers and, at low tide, it was possible to walk under a natural arch to the shoreline 'below Bloodstone' Hill. George had warned us about collecting too many geological specimens, for there would be a long slog on the return, and the pathside was littered with the fragments of rock jettisoned by those who, not long before, had enthusiastically gathered them.

We looked for specimens of bloodstone, which was beloved by the Victorians, who mined it commercially. In the nineteenth century, the red-flecked stone from this hill was fashioned into jewellery. It was enough, bearing George's warning in mind, to take some photographs of specimens of bloodstone, having first dipped them in the sea to wet them and improve the clarity.

On the return to Kinloch that evening, we kept pace with a middle-aged couple. He was an academic and most taciturn; she prattled on, drawing no response from her husband. 'All my husband can think about just now is waves,' said the lady, and we were silent, waiting for the explanation. 'Waves! In the bath! At the castle!' Then we recalled the exquisite fittings in the bathroom and especially the bath cum shower, encased in fine hardwood, with a door concealing the complex plumbing and knobs to control the temperature and flow of the water. There was one knob marked 'Waves', a boon to anyone who found pleasure in sailing a toy boat while having a bath!

Ian's speciality was organising a ceilidh. Refreshments consisted of whatever the people took along, the drinks ranging from coke to whisky. Recorded music was played for dancing of the lusty Scottish variety, as typified by 'The Dashing White Sergeant'. It was a relaxed atmosphere, with someone playing the Northumbrian pipes and others the violin and flutes. Ian would sing and visitors would provide something special, such as a song about Rum. The following was written by archaeologists and intended to be sung to the strains of 'My Favourite Things' from *The Sound of Music*:

Red deer and ponies and tractors that rattle;
NCC wardens and black Highland cattle;
Black and white sea birds that come here to nest—
These are the things about Rum we love best.

Chorus:
When the clegs bite
When the wind blows
When you want to curse—
We simply remember what we're here to do
And that makes us feel much worse.

When we're digging or wet-sieving
And we're feeling numb
Despite all the weather
We've had since we came—
We all like it here on Rum!

Verse 2
Looking for bloodstone we find entertaining:
Waking each morning to see that it's raining—
Mud in your wellies and soil in your vest,
These are the things about Rum we like best.

Chorus
Verse 3
Watching sea eagles that soar over ridges,
Looking for benchmarks that should be on bridges;
Dreaming of midges that give you no rest—
These are the things about Rum we love best.

Chorus

Verse 4
Wild goats in sea caves that frighten the walkers;
Land Rovers packed to the gunnels with stalkers,
All here to look at red deer at their best—
These are the things about Rum we love best.

Chorus

John Betjeman loved the Edwardian grandeur of Kinloch Castle. I marvelled at its rosy hue, which contrasted with the full greys of the rock elsewhere on the island. Sir George—who had prospered in Lancashire as a manufacturer of textile machines and was 'not short of a bob or two', as they say in those parts—arranged for boatloads of sandstone to be imported from Arran. He also contrived to bring up Lancashire workers and insisted on them wearing kilts, which are not to be recommended during the midge season.

When the Nature Conservancy acquired the island and its properties, they planned to restore a sheep-degraded habitat and to study and manage the red deer. It was always a delight to tour the Castle, passing the grand piano, one of the best in Scotland, and coming under the beady gaze of mounted deer. The hall was decked with oddities collected by the Bulloughs during their extensive tours in the Far East. I used to marvel at the three-ton bronze eagle in its own turret room.

Members of the British Deer Society used to stay in the Castle and one midnight, just before we turned in, George began operating the huge electric-powered organ that was fitted under the grand staircase and worked on the pianola system. The (wheezy) strains of Wagner must have terrified anyone who had already gone to bed!

Hallival was the first of the Rum peaks to fall to us, mainly because at breakfast-time, as George looked out of the window at Ian and Kathy's house, Hallival was in such clear view he could see a splinter of rock sticking from the upper slopes. He was determined to find that rock—and to climb it!

Breakfast was a substantial meal, partaken at a circular table, which Kathy had decked with knife, fork, spoon and as usual, binoculars: several pairs of binoculars this time, in case there was a red-throated diver to be seen on Loch Scresort, or one of the golden eagles was beating the bounds. Ian told us of the cat that had stalked a cuckoo—and how the bird flew off minus one or two tail feathers. He said that a pair of corncrakes were nesting in the tangled vegetation near the house and we kept a close watch while we ate, hoping for a grandstand view of one of the birds.

We packed our rucksacks and sprayed waterproofing on our boots, sending a wraith of cigarette smoke into the clear island air; we then set off to find the path, which began in the sodden area behind the Castle—an area where the midges lived and from which they emerged in brown clouds when the weather conditions suited them. Ian had heard of midge larvae being found many feet down in the peat, so there seemed little chance of the stock being reduced by severe winter weather. The midges of Rum are so tough they fly sorties in the rain, and it has been said that if you destroy one midge, then 1,000 will attend its funeral!

The path from Kinloch to the summit of Askival, via Hallival, offers little respite. We were conscious of passing through different zones, from the moorland, with its ling and sphagnum, to arid areas where the stagshorn seemed to be one of only a few plants capable of surviving, by dint of keeping its head down and its rootstock long, questing for moisture.

George did find his rock; he did climb it, and a record was kept of the ascent. Not surprisingly, he could see Ian's house from the top! Anyone who climbed Hallival with George was photographed in a death-defying situation—where a rock was wedged across a gorge that looked to be 1,000 feet deep. The idea was for two people to shake hands over the void. The trick was to take a picture from such an angle that the viewer would not be aware that the gash was only about a dozen feet deep, and would see only the deep glen beyond and far below!

We walked to the 'lawns' which brought welcome patches of verdant green to the mountain top. They were to be found in the vicinity of burrows that were the nesting places of Manx shearwaters. The droppings of the birds provided fertilisation, and the shortness of the grass was a testimony to the persistent grazing by red deer. I shall never forget the sense of wonder I felt when I reached the summit of Hallival, expecting an absence of life, only to be told by George that under my feet were hundreds of seabirds, squatting in their burrows, incubating eggs at the start of a prolonged nesting season.

The Manx shearwater—so named because it was first closely studied on the Isle of Man—is two-tone: dark grey above, white beneath. It has a tubular bill and a faint musty odour. This species of shearwater is an inexhaustible traveller, nesting on the western seaboard of Europe and wintering off the coast of South America. Birds of the year have appeared in Brazilian waters a few weeks after leaving the nesting burrows of the Hebrides and Wales. This was established by the recovery of light aluminium rings that had been placed on the legs of birds before they were capable of flight.

The Manx shearwater conserves energy by gliding for long periods, using the upthrust of air from the waves. While one of a pair remains in the burrow on Rum, the other goes off to feed, sometimes as far as the Bay of Biscay, for distance is no object to such a master bird of the air.

The shearwaters fly by night while their main enemies, the big gulls, are roosting, but eagles also prey on the birds, striking them either at first light or when there is a moon. The mortality of young birds is considerable, and some perish during the vital first, flightless journey to the sea. It has been known for the helpless birds to arrive at the village of Kinloch, where they are rescued from cats and kept overnight by friendly villagers, to be released by Loch Scresort on the following day. A scientist who was using a mercury-vapour lamp on the Castle lawn had to discontinue his work of catching moths when more than a hundred shearwaters alighted round about the lamp.

The western cliffs of Rum were the setting for a scientific test of George's walking ability. He was so often ahead of us that, when we stopped for a snack, we surreptitiously slipped a few chuckies (rocks) in his rucksack. He shouldered it and moved off. More chuckies were added at the next stop. George grunted a little when picking up the bag but he resumed the walk uncomplainingly. We had correctly assessed how many chuckies would be needed, for now his pace matched ours!

Easter Sunday was our big day on the island; it involved a 15-mile expedition from Harris, the former crofting settlement in the south-west. We would walk round the back of Ruinsival, up to Ainshval, into Glen Dibidil and back to Kinloch by the coastal walk. Ian drove us along the rocky road to Harris, passing the area where the sea eaglets brought from Scandinavia were kept and fed until they could be confidently released. We saw Highland cattle, fearsome-looking with their long horns but docile by nature—the descendants of cattle brought from the mainland in a chartered landing craft. And we saw deer—the celebrated red deer of Rum, now tattered with the moult of the winter coat, the big stags beginning to grow new sets of antlers behind the hairy skin we know as 'velvet'.

We visited the 'Grecian temple' on the deer-cropped sward by the roaring Atlantic. Originally, the Bulloughs were to be interred in a chamber excavated in a nearby hillside. The face of the mausoleum was tiled and the body of Sir George's father was reverently placed here. Then a friend of the family, looking at the tiling, compared it with a city toilet, and Sir George, distressed, had the new mausoleum built in classic form. Here, where the breezes come direct from the New World and where each spring parties of· golden plover rest up for a few days before proceeding on migratory flight to Iceland and other points north, the remains of father, son and wife lie in peace.

George tells a story of how, when Lady Bullough died in the South, her body was transported to Kinloch for interment. She who had been an Edwardian beauty was now—er—somewhat corpulent.

There was a wish that the islanders might bear her body across Rum for interment at Harris, but they contrived by night to put the body in a boat and take it round by sea, to be spared the gruelling journey overland!

On our journey to southern Rum, I had my first view of Papidil (named after Celtic priests). Sir George had a lodge made there among trees by a freshwater loch. The lodge is now ruined, and we heard that someone had ventured ashore from a large boat and removed many of the slates. A friend in Yorkshire recalls visiting the island many years ago and discovering the lodge, which he preferred to his tent. So he slept in comparative luxury. At that time, the heating system worked, so he collected driftwood, stoked up the boiler and had the luxury of a bath within hearing of the sea and under the wondering gaze of the wild goats and their kids, who had not previously seen smoke pouring from the building.

We had our first butty stop (snack meal) overlooking Papidil and the shimmering sea. In view was Muck, Ardnamurchan Point, the island of Coll and the Dutchman's Cap.

Five wild goats lay in the sunshine at the tousled rim of our island. Sir George imported some goats, where they joined up with that ancient stock seen and commented on by Pennant in 1772. On the cliffs the goats can remain cool and be free from the summer torment of insect pests. Sea breezes also waft away the strong body odours of the billies during the rut. A friend claims that a wild goat always moves into the wind to avoid its own rancid smell!

The hoarse voices of ravens led us to scan the sky—and to locate one of the white-tailed sea eagles which, with its immense wings spanning some eight feet, has been likened to a flying barn door. The eagle cruised fairly low; showing off the white tail of maturity and vanishing round the hill end.

We plodded up a desert of weathered boulders, then over mossy ground, where we came under the scrutiny of a red hind and her last year's calf. Halfway up the slope, we heard the twittering of swallows and saw our first 'blue birds' of the year, They were hawking insects at an elevation of about 2,000 feet.

As we neared the summit of Ainshval, another sea eagle came into view; it had allowed a thermal to carry it high, where it was gliding in a broad spiral against a cloudless sky. The sunshine revealed the fine details of its plumage. Later, hearing a ringing call, we were directed to where an eagle was gliding towards Muck. And later still, as we negotiated a scree slope, two eagles were seen to be occupying rock turrets on the vast cliff of Ainshval.

From the hill, we looked across at the Cuillins of Rum and those of Skye; we saw the smooth grey-blue forms of the outer islands, like a school of whales, in line ahead. Sixty miles away to the east, Ben Nevis was visible, presiding over its retinue of lesser hills.

Our original plan had been to traverse Trollival and the two bealachs leading to a steep direct descent to Kinloch, but the sun was beginning to descend towards the western horizon. We emulated the goats and went over the edge—onto the scree slopes and the pocket-handkerchief-sized tufts of grass. Our feet encountered rocks that had been smoothed by wind and rain or cracked by quick changes of temperature. We descended diagonally, amid a clatter of stones and with minor oaths as our feet slithered or squelched. We had time to stop and admire Askival and Hallival, now pinkish in the late evening sunlight.

After the scree slope we came across more coarse grass, rank heather, boulder and bog, until the path to the Dibidil hut was beneath our feet. Our way lay across the foaming burn. With increasing weariness we followed the undulations of the path along the eastern side of Rum. Fulmars croaked and male grouse crowed; the bass baritone voices of greater black-backed gulls came from the rock stacks. Hinds and calves were rimmed by light from a low-slung sun.

A red-throated diver appeared high up, having doubtless left a hill lochan. The bird moved strongly, then cut off the power source and went into a shallow glide, touching down on the sea about a quarter of a mile away. (Ian later told us that he had heard the wind strumming the partly-closed wings of divers gliding down to feed in Loch Scresort.)

Back at the home of the Simpsons, Kathie delighted us with some well-cooked venison. She had used a prime cut from a stag and put the meat in the oven 12 hours before we ate it. She believes that venison should be cooked slowly and she does not drench it with sauces.

With an anti-cyclone centred on the North Sea, the Hebrides were at the edge, attracting cloud, mist and rain. Next morning we left Kinloch at 9.30 a.m., and less than three hours later stood on Fiunchro, at around 2,000 feet. It was an honest climb, from sea level, and a hard one, over generally soft ground. The only sound heard on the ascent was a golden plover's sad aria. As a dalesman, I missed the bleating of sheep. Rum has no sheep.

Now we stood on Fiunchro, on a patch of level ground, with the mist so thick we could taste it. We decided to have our snack meal, and minutes later herring gulls appeared from the cloying vapour and circled the area. How did they know we were at that moment unpacking sandwiches? Could they hear the crackling of greaseproof paper?

Sometime during the night, the weather changed. We awoke to sunlight. The wind became a balmy breeze. The *Pioneer* collected us and we cruised on the sound between Rum and Eigg, with our escort of Manx shearwaters. They appeared in large groups, hundreds of birds passing low over the water and overhauling the craft without difficulty for we were doing a modest ten knots. At Eigg, the shearwaters handed over to Arctic terns, which showed off their snow-white plumage against a uniformly blue sky.

The Island seemed lovelier than ever, with a turquoise sea lapping against white sands and the northern moors an intense and dramatic purple hue. The Gaelic name for Eigg is Eilean Eige, or 'isle of the notch', referring to its central V-shaped glen. Macculloch, a nineteenth-century visitor, insisted it came from 'eg' or edge, referring to the island's single most stupendous feature—the Sgurr, which rears up like an immense mane, striated vertically and capped at 900 feet by a block of pitchstone lava. I once entertained the fantastic thought that it had been towed here from Nevada.

We carried our heavy packs through daisy-covered fields to the Manse, where the Minister's wife provided us with coffee. Then we moved northwards to see the ruined kirk and the Celtic cross with a top propped up against the base since it was struck by lightning. Bluebells edged the fields and the cliffs. The *Pioneer*, heading for Mallaig across the Sound of Sleat, seemed a small boat on a very big sea.

So much for the sunny side of Eigg; in the west, mist boiled over the Cleadale cliffs like steam rising from a cauldron.

We were impressed by the floral richness—by the profusion of primroses, orchids and the patches of moss campion. Normally, the view would have taken in mountainous Rum. We stared, instead, at clammy mist—'wet as a dishcloth', as Fred said—and while eating our sandwiches, listened to the ravens conversing and gazed at the place where the edge of the cliff showed dark against the cloying vapour. Fred pointed to a silhouette of our gracious Queen Victoria!

The Minister under whose roof we stayed hailed from Harris, where his aged mother 'thinks in Gaelic but writes letters in English'. At the time of our visit, his black cow had come into season and he was anxious to recruit a bull to ensure genetic continuation.

Leaving him to his farming activities, we sauntered forth, to the sound of cuckoos perched on shrub or telegraph pole. We found a plastic sack and began to pick up the rusting beer cans that lay within throwing distance of the road. The sack was soon filled and the sun glinted on thousands more tins. George proposed that we climb the Sgurr which, from the direction of the Manse, looked like some monstrous film set, unscalable.

'Och, nae problem,' said George, and sauntered round the back where a track acceptable to goats led to a gully and from here up and up to the summit of a rock, where a rusting metal bar appeared to be acting as a television aerial for someone down below.

The Minister happily combined his religious activities with something akin to crofting, using the church's few acres. On Sunday morning, he went out to milk his cow, taking his radio with him so as to listen to the weather forecast. That day he planned to minister to the Christians of the island of Muck. The departure of 'the Muck boat' was a highlight of the week. The Minister had hired the craft from the doctor's son, who normally used it for fishing. The doctor turned up, and would visit each of his patients on Muck whether or not they required his services.

The Minister was clad in Sabbath black, his daughter wearing an outfit of soft russet tints, complete with bonnet. I imagined it to have been knitted by lamplight on a wild winter evening. The doctor wore a kilt. There was the obligatory dirk tucked into one of his stockings.

The boat, breathing blue exhaust smoke, left the sheltering rocks of Eigg; it was comforting to see that we were towing a dinghy. As we neared the island, waves were destroying themselves in a mass of foam on an exposed reef. The boatman, staying well out, followed the line of the shore until the white, gable end of a cottage on Muck appeared from behind a low cliff; the boat was then confidently turned and driven between foam-crested rocks towards Port Mor, under the gaze of cormorant, shag, eider and black guillemot. We were welcomed to Muck by a visitor—from Yorkshire!

Muck, smallest of the island group, seemed to have a struggle to keep above water level. Low, fringed by rocks, it was a mere three miles long, but, being a basaltic island, had good soil, a mild climate, and an enviable reputation for early potatoes..

The name is said to be an anglicised version of the Gaelic for 'sea pig', surely a reference to seals. Grey seals haul up here for pupping, though Muck does not have a large colony. Another possibility is that Muck is derived from Muc Mara, a reference to the dolphin, seen while on passage.

We walked through the Deserted Village, a northern Pompeii. This roofless complex was destroyed by time, having been built by displaced crofters early last century and vacated not long afterwards. Cheviot sheep, with lambs at foot, were grazing locally. We had a snack meal lying in the sun on a knoll above the white-sand beach near Horse Island. Across the sands strode the doctor from Eigg, on his round of patients. He was a solitary figure in the austere landscape; he left a conspicuous track as he crossed the tide-smoothed sands.

Fred, spying a telephone on Muck, put in a transfer charge call to his wife. He heard her voice, followed by the voice of the operator asking if she would pay for the call. Its origin was queried. 'Muck,' said the helpful operator. Said Fred's wife: 'I beg your pardon...'

There was time to watch the birds. Oystercatchers, those vociferous pied pipers, gave life to the tideline. Some herring gulls had their nests, on lichen-plated rocks in an area where most other rocks would go under water at high tide. We located an eider, which had covered her nest like a feathered tea cosy.

On our return to Eigg, we carried chickens in boxes. Next morning, at 6.15, there was a great to-do among the hens at the Manse as the new chickens were initiated into the Manse flock through prolonged and noisy rites aimed at having them accepted. I admired the Minister's patience.

It was on Eigg that George demonstrated his ability to light a fire with a sandwich paper, using some apparently sodden fish boxes and debris picked up from a beach being swept by heavy rain. We were near the Singing Sands, having walked up through Cleadale, where an old man had recalled for us how his family used to cook shearwaters. These ocean-going birds nest on the cliffs behind the tiny houses. George insisted that we should walk where the sands were known to sing, and this we did, scuffing them with our boots to the accompaniment of strange noises—squeals rather than lullabies. We were later to hear that the Gaelic name of this area—Camas Sgiotaig— refers to the way the sand disperses in winter, when the storms rage. The sand is invariably brought back by the flow tides in spring!

The Singing Sands utter their shrill squeaking when the grains—which are uniform in size—have been dampened. Hugh Miller, in *The Cruise of the Betsey*, published in 1858, made the first mention in print of the Sounding Sand of Eigg. 'I struck it obliquely with my foot, where the surface lay dry... and... elicited a shrill sonorous note.' He repeated the action, 'and with every blow the shrill note was repeated. My companion joined me: and we performed a concert which, if we could boast of but little variety in the tones produced, might at least challenge all Europe for an instrument of the kind which produced them.'

On the day of our visit, we lamented over the quantity of tideborne rubbish that disfigured the area. The restless sea had brought in most objects from a plastic bag to a telegraph pole, the latter from a deck cargo swept overboard in heavy seas. (We were to find a small cove on Sanday, off Canna, jammed with telegraph poles.)

Sheltering from the rain under an overhang on the main cliff we had our snack meal. 'Och, but let's have a fire,' said George. We watched, enthralled, as he crumpled up a sandwich paper. Then, picking up part of a fish box, he used his knife to produce shavings of wood, which he carefully spread over the paper. So fine were the shavings, they soon caught fire.

The size and bulk of material was increased as the fire took hold. I watched George hurl onto the flames pieces of fish box, then whole fish boxes. In a frenzy of tidiness, we picked up plastic objects and incinerated them. George, who had begun with a match against a piece of sandwich paper, now contemplated burning a telegraph pole.

We returned to Mallaig on a sun-flecked sea, recalling our first ventures across the Sound of Sleat with Brucie Watts in his boat *The Western Isles*. Brucie was a veteran of the angry sea, his boat spending much of its life with a flurry of waves about it. George remembered a wild February morning when he and some other deer-watchers, hopeful of reaching Rum, strode down to Mallaig harbour, with the wind howling between the telephone wires and the sky inky-black. He climbed aboard *The Western Isles*, thumped a foot on the deck, and waited till a tousled Brucie appeared.

'Are we goin' to Rum, Brucie?' asked George.

Brucie looked into the blackest part of the sky. 'Och, aye,' he replied, 'I think it's clearin' a bit.' And off they went, with the few passengers too busy holding on to the superstructure to be sick...

8 A CROW ON THE TABLE
The Isle of Skye

I awoke to the cry of a herring gull. It made the area ring with its laughing calls and then subsided into a chuckle. The sun leaped into a clear sky and the radio weather forecaster promised more good weather.

I looked across the channel between the Kyle of Lochalsh and Skye and reassured myself that the island had not drifted away during the night. I lay on the bed, listening to music by Elgar and reading some purple prose from the hotel brochure:

> The lochs are the blue of chalcedony, the gorse on grassy banks a blaze of gold on green and, in the long evenings, mountains take on a blue haze. There is something about the stillness of a Highland evening, when the curlew calls and a lazy ribbon of peat smoke from crofter's cottage brings that comforting tangy smell to you on the clear, clean air.

I quietly sobbed—until the ramp of the Skye ferry dropped with a clang some 50 yards from the hotel window; until air brakes hissed and another lorry lumbered towards the ferry; and until that wretched herring gull went through its repertoire of ringing cries.

It was to be an expedition to Skye with a difference: we would stay on the mainland and fit in some mainland sights as well, such as Beinn Bhan, overlooking the high pass to Applecross.

We would rid ourselves of car stiffness on this huge expanse of Torridonian Sandstone. It was rather like walking through a painted desert, for the rose-red rock held a multi-hued array of lichen. Stagshorn protruded like miniature cacti in this arid part of Old Caledonia. The rainless weeks meant that-the vegetation was crunchy underfoot.

We cheated, of course, parking the car beside the Pass at over 2,000 feet. The view took in a shining sea and blue islands. The only clouds were of the billowing cumulus variety, tethered to the Cuillins of Skye. On our way to the summit of Beinn Bhan we passed through this strange, disordered desert of rock in many shapes but only one hue—the dull red of a firebrick, as though the landscape had set in terror. Other features were perched boulders and boulder slopes—potential ankle-wreckers—with expanses of leggy heather about them.

Fred's monopoly of drinking water, which he had hoped to exploit for financial gain, came to an end when his brother, Ron, discovered a spring. The packed lunch contained part of a grapefruit, chicken and beef, with salad, a roll, apple and—a strawberry. We consumed it with the help of plastic cutlery, in the blistering heat of an untypical Highland day. The food attracted what must have been the season's first bumble bee.

We made rapid progress on higher ground, walking to the rim of a valley the sides of which plunged for more than 1,000 feet. We slogged to the skyline, through typical ptarmigan country, with the clink of loose stones underfoot. Our reward was to stand on the rim of a precipice some 2,000 feet high, the edge crusted with snow. We looked across half of Scotland!

That evening, in the hotel lounge, George—fresh from work in the Middle East—showered us with Camel cigarettes, Havana cigars and small coins bearing the outlines of palm trees. Fred switched the attention back to Scotland—more specifically to Skye—by recalling a social event at Portree, many years before, when one of the whisky-drinkers, feeling excessively thirsty, suddenly picked up a vase of daffodils, threw away the flowers and drank the water. Fred asked a girl to dance. 'It took me three laps of the dance floor to catch up with her.'

I smiled at the story of the Southern lady who wrote to the ferry company asking to book a berth from the Kyle of Lochalsh to Skye—a voyage of just a few minutes. Skye achieved considerable romance through its association with Bonnie Prince Charlie, and the huddled rock turrets of the Cuillins distinguish the southern part of the island. Immense numbers of people visit Skye in summer and gather at one or two 'honeypots', including Dunvegan Castle; George said he would take us to the Quiraing, where we would be looking for a rather special Table.

Skye, 'The Misty Isle', was at its sunny best. It was disappointing to see peat-diggers wearing blue overalls instead of tartaned clothes. North of Portree, a joiner was reconstructing a sheep-fank. At Staffin, where the tide rolled in to wash the sand in a half-moon shaped bay, were black-faced sheep with new lambs. A crofting house was being renovated—with breeze-blocks.

The Cuillins of Skye are for the bold and the brawny. In the north-east of the island, where the Trotternish—a playground of ravens—rears itself boldly against the skyline, are rocks with strong verticals, in particular the Old Man of Storr, at the southern end. This Old Man, some 160 feet high, stands at a gravity-defying angle. In the north is the Pillared Stronghold, here translated from Cuith-raing, which became the Quiraing and is pronounced Cooraing. George had often spoken to us about the fabulous Quiraing.

The instability of the cliffs led to the formation of impressive corries, castellations, pillars and steep and narrow ravines. The best of the pinnacles was given an inappropriate name—the Needle. Its height is 100 feet and it looks unsafe. At the centre of the Quiraing is a crag with a flattish top—the Table. The rock round about is dark, but the heart of the Quiraing is always bright, for the table is covered by a 'cloth' of green— by the short springy grass that can thrive in such an upland situation.

George, not seeing an obvious parking space near the Quiraing, simply drove his car onto the moor, braking near a peat-hag, to the surprise of a cock wheatear. Halfway to the skyline we had our packed meal—another elaborate offering by the hotel, the meal including smoked mackerel.

On, then, to the grand canyons of Skye—to one of the steep and narrow gullies between high rock walls leading, we hoped, to the Table: the rock which, as George reminded us for the umpteenth time, is topped by grass so short and green it might be of baize. Our first effort was in a gully that was slippery and soon attained the vertical. Any displaced stones came close to producing a sonic boom as they passed the people lower down. Three of us retreated; George and Ian continued and were last seen clinging to some rocks like roosting bats.

The next gully seemed more promising. We encountered screes and sandy bits, but also many grassy ledges. Cracks in the cliffs had been colonised by purple saxifrage. The Table stood in a natural amphitheatre, with pinnacles to provide special effects. Where were George and Ian? A bearded walker appeared with two dogs. He said he thought two men were 'stuck' in a gully. Then our adventurers appeared. George said they had such a struggle, 'I'm sure we climbed halfway up a bloody stack.'

We slithered from the Table to the 100-foot column of rock that is the other notable feature of Quiraing. And all the time there was a dispute between ravens carrying twigs and crows with 'chips' on their shoulders. A crow stooped at a twig-bearing raven. Birds flew around each other.

We heard the deep croaking of the ravens and the honking of the crows.

Next day, a mainland outing to the Falls of Glomach turned out to be a bruising expedition with eight miles on track and estate road and two miles of track on a steep hillside. A guide book writer had noted: 'For the arduous ascent to these falls, stout footwear and abundant energy are essential' Our reward was the sight of one of the highest waterfalls in Britain.

We arrived in Glen Eichaig, a few miles from Eilean Donan Castle, on what a local man called the first day of spring. Riverside flats were greening up. A vivid green on the birks was that of new leaves. A wavering chevron of grey geese passed overhead. The red deer, which had presumably been on the riverside during the night, were now quietly working their way back up the hill, where they would lie quietly during the day. Across our path went some blocky stags and lean, lithe hinds. Two stags sparred, rearing up on their hind legs to 'box' with the forelegs, as they do when antlers have been cast.

Deering was forgotten with the appearance of two golden eagles in gliding flight which carried them effortlessly over a ridge, not far from where a cliff sprouted a mountain pine. It was the type of isolated big tree on which eagles like to nest.

We selected ground that looked tick-free and ate our mid-day snack while a nestling crow called repeatedly from a conifer. Three Irish lads who had visited the Falls came bouncing down the main track. They had not a stitch of clothing above the waist and we shuddered at the thought of all the ticks that had hitched a lift.

The Falls are seen only by the persistent walker for they lie in a side valley and are approached on goat-tracks, nothing more, in an area of green ridges, crags, boulder slopes and peaty burns. The main watercourse is so deeply-sunk in the landscape it is not often glimpsed by visitors. Halfway through the walk, the topmost waterfall can be seen. For viewing the whole mighty spectacle, it is necessary to descend to a beaten-down patch near the gully.

We watched the water racing down the upper glen; it flowed over permanently wet rocks and seethed on the wet stones far, far below.

A recurrent problem during our Highland excursions was pronouncing Gaelic names. Fred did well with Beinn Sgritheall, pronouncing it 'skreel'. Someone asked: 'Why couldn't they say so in the first place?' Getting to the top proved to be another energetic activity. We had a guide, a member of the local Mountain Rescue Team, complete with two search dogs. She carried a radio and was in contact with the rescue service. On that day, we had a code name—Dog 5.

As we left the car, under the eyes of a circling buzzard, the skyline route was pointed out: it looked brutal. We shared the hill with some red deer. One of them had cast an antler which it had chewed in a bid to regain lost calcium. Packed lunch was taken as we snuggled among the grey boulders at 2,600 feet. The wind was eye-wateringly cold; it rustled our anoraks and the plastic containers containing smoked salmon and other goodies.

The ground became so steep, so rocky, that we approached the summit on hands and knees. Our reward was a breathtaking view, including the Five Sisters of Kintail and the islands south of Skye. The awesome northern cliffs of Canna appeared. We looked immediately down on Loch Hourn, and on mountains that appeared to spring from the water, as in a Norwegian fjord. George promised to take us to Loch Hourn—and he would borrow a boat for the expedition. A few flakes of snow drifted by as we beheld this remote area.

We called up the Mountain Rescue base and a cheerful voice inquired if we had seen any foxes. We had had our noses so close to the ground on the climb that we could not have looked around. We gave up-to-date reports on other walkers.

As we returned to Kyle, six wild goats crossed the road and scurried between the birks. At 11.15 p.m., Ian, who was presiding over a wee party in his bedroom, rang up Fred and said, 'Dog 5 calling...' From Fred came the words: 'Dog-tired replying...'

We returned to Skye. The bonnet of our car pointed towards the Cuillin Hills, which we approached via Broadford and Elgol. We had a breathtaking view of the Cuillins which, tightly grouped, in various shades of blue and grey, cast their reflections in the calm sea. Wheatears and stonechats were vocal and lively on the rough ground we passed at the start of a 12-mile walk to and from Sligachan, by way of Camasunary. Down on the beach, with a washed-up telegraph pole as a seat, we ate our snack meal and looked across a sparkling sea towards Eigg and Rum. The bay had two far-reaching headlands and on the water floated guillemot and red-throated diver. Gulls and oystercatchers inhabited the tide's edge. Turning round, I looked over the close-cropped turf to where a party of northern golden plover were resting on their migratory journey, possibly to Iceland.

The Cuillins, alone in this wild landscape, had cloud about them and flakes of snow swirling in the fierce draughts. The cloud looked like steam rising from a dark cauldron. Yet we walked in sunshine and it was hurtful to the eyes to look for too long at the silvered sea. At closer quarters, we shivered and donned a few more clothes. We entered the gap between Sgurr na Stri and Strathaird, with 3,000-foot hills rising about us in jagged peaks. The water we saw was an arm of the sea, but we had the impression it was landlocked—a lochan, indeed— and in it was an islet formed of gabbro, thinly thatched with heather. The mist and rain was sufficient to nourish a strong vegetational growth in cracks and crannies.

A party of walkers was negotiating the Bad Step, a terrible initiation to the Cuillins from this direction. A faulty step here results in a ducking. The walkers had no mishaps and went purposefully on...

9 THROUGH THE JAWS OF HELL
Loch Hourn

'Nay problem,' said George, referring to his promise to take us to Loch Hourn with car and boat. We had presented ourselves at his home on Kinnoull Hill at Perth. John quietly mentioned the absence of a boat and also of a car with a tow-bar. 'Nae problem,' we were told.

George telephoned a friend and returned to announce 'The boat's arranged.' He drove off in his car and returned with a Land-Rover that had about it the far-from-subtle smell of farm manure. 'Och, it's a healthy smell,' he said.

We asked no further questions hut simply stowed away in the Land-Rover some of our gear and provisions; including two members of the haggis clan (twa haggi?). George drove into town and collected a boat from a friend who, an hour before, had not known about our trip; when he returned we loaded the remaining food and gear onto the boat. The trailer creaked in protest.

Then away we went—to the Great Glen, with a stop at Invergarry for petrol and at Tomdoun for wee drammies for the lads. We then faced some 40 miles in a Highland cul-de-sac. The road unfolded in long, straight stretches. The celestial hosepipe was turned full on and we felt sorry for the red deer that looked so cold and bedraggled in a wild stretch of country that did not appear to offer them a single blade of green grass. One stag resorted to the moose-like tactic of sinking its head in a lochan to dine on aquatic weed.

While chatting with a ghillie we noticed that his dog was bleeding at the throat. Said the ghillie, with verbal economy: 'The tick!' His dog, while romping through dead and draggled bracken, had picked up a sheep-tick—the curse o' the Heilands.

The road passed within caber-tossing distance of Loch Quoich (pronounce it 'coo-ick') and George recalled that he once had a day's fishing there. 'The only things that were moving were the boat and a bottle of whisky.' John looked disappointed. 'Och,' said George, 'the wee troots in the burns around Kinloch Hourn queue up to take the bait. And if they don't, we can always nip down to Fort William for fish suppers!' The idea of 'nipping' anywhere from remote Loch Hourn was preposterous, as George well knew.

The road to Loch Hourn dipped between rock outcrops and walls lagged with moss. We journeyed beside a thundering burn. The countryside steamed like an old-fashioned kitchen on wash-day. Then the road straightened out. Ahead of us, beside the loch, was the huddle of buildings we sought.

'I told you there'd be nae problems,' said George.

We arrived at Kinloch Hourn on the last day of winter. In the Highlands, you can forget clocks and calendars: go by what you see and smell and hear. Our arrival was on a depressingly wet, chilly day, with the burns in full spate, the red deer huddled in the glen and the trees looking as lifeless as telegraph poles. A wind came howling up from the loch as though trying to find a way out.

On the following morning, we saw the gleam of sunshine. Glorious spring-like weather followed. The roar of the burn became a. whisper, the deer went up the hill—leaving their antlers behind them—and the trees burst into fresh young leaf.

We were staying in a 'wee bothy' and were welcomed to it by a black cat which (we later discovered) had been born on a boat in Mallaig harbour and since its arrival at Kinloch Hourn had become related to every cat in the district.

John formed a special affection for Cheeky the cat whereas Fred merely tolerated the animal and George showed some hostility, especially when he saw Cheeky prowling in the kitchen. And who could blame him? We fed Cheeky outdoors. John had the cat in mind when he took his rod and line to the lochans and burns looking for trout. The fish, like Cheeky, were invariably on short rations in the gin-clear, acid water; they almost savaged any lure that John used, and once—when he attached a spinner to the line—he gasped when he saw a wee trout pursuing this shiny object which, in truth, was larger than itself! Cheeky was absent one day. John, inconsolable, believed it had impaled itself on a fish bone. Next morning, the cat had returned, large as life, and licked itself over while waiting for some sign of life in the kitchen.

The bothy was in classic Scottish style—two ee's (eyes— windows) and a moo' (mouth—door). Fred and John took over the upstairs bedroom, the bothy having had dormer windows added, and they rejoiced in their good fortune until, being in a small room with a big window and flimsy curtains, they were awakened by the brightness of the new day and found it difficult to sleep again.

George slung his bag onto the bed in the front downstairs bedroom and rejoiced—until, at first light, ponies congregated immediately outside to be fed. Being a lover of fresh air, George had left the window partly open and awoke to see the head of a pony extended into the room.

I had the remaining—the back—bedroom and went to bed with a view through the window of the black cat curled upon the window ledge, and of the moonlit hill beyond. I had no disturbance after the clank of the dustbin lid marked the arrival of the hungry neighbourhood badger.

At this bothy the kitchen had been added, apparently as an afterthought, and beyond that was another lean-to roofed with corrugated iron, to house the wood and coal. The living room was heated by a coal fire; a backboiler was fitted and the draught was such that I thought the roar of the fire would be heard in the next glen. It was a snug lodging. The living-room walls were lined with wood, unadorned by pictures or ornaments—until George hung up a cast antler he had found on the hill.

At first, some 'fettling' was necessary. We had a clothes line but no pegs, so George fashioned some from spare wire taken from the fence. No axe was provided so we chopped up wood for kindling using the edge of a roofing slate. The living room carpet looked a little dusty, so we took it out of doors and shook it, beat it, dragged it over the dewy grass, let it dry, beat it again and returned it to the floor of the room. A visiting ghillie stared in amazement. 'Och,' he said, 'ye shouldna brought your own carpet.'

There was indeed a spirit of remoteness at Kinloch Hourn. It turned out that the ponies were used for trekking, which seemed appropriate to this wild setting. We met a man who was living in an amphibious vehicle which had reached the loch in virtually a straight line from Mallaig.

George's grand plan had been to motor to Mallaig. Here we would leave the car and take to the boat, crossing the sound to the mouth of Loch Hourn. Fred urged him to think again. What he actually said was: 'You're bloody mad.' The boat, put in the water for the first time at Kinloch Hourn, floated for a short time and then began to fill with water. We dragged it back on the beach and, shamefacedly, put in the plug! We launched it again. George coaxed life into the engine. We cruised on calm water that carried a mirror-image of the hills.

In Gaelic mythology, Loch Hourn is a haunt of the Devil. The name is said to be derived from 'Iutharn', meaning Hell. I began to think of it as a heavenly place.

We followed a cattle trod that began where the beasts scrambled ashore after swimming the narrows of Kylde Rhea, between Skye and Glenelg, and then were driven beside Loch Hourn towards Lochaber. Cattle that were sold at the Lowland Trysts continued their journey into England. I have heard the Scottish cattle being referred to in Teesdale as 'kyloes', doubtless from the kyles they swam from their native islands to the mainland.

Thomas Pennant, that perceptive eighteenth-century visitor to the Highlands, recorded how the rough drovers subsisted on oatmeal and onions which they mixed with blood taken from one of the living cattle. The drovers were clad in woven or knitted wool. I fancy they carried a haversack, for the oatmeal that was made into haverbread. In Yorkshire I heard from an old man how the mixture was sometimes made in a shallow hole in the ground. When the drover s appetite was satisfied, his dog ate up the remaining food!

John, the angler, was soon in action. I do not think he expected to catch anything in deep water with the boat travelling in a spirited fashion. His attention then switched to an island, Eilean Mhogh-sgeir, which looked craggy in parts and elsewhere was luxuriant with heather, blueberry and small trees. Herons were nesting in a tree at the eastern end. John, having tried several times to pronounce the Gaelic name, began to call this plot of ground Heron Island.

As we landed, we came under the steady gaze of a mallard on her nest in the heather. A young stag, which had swum from the mainland to enjoy a plentiful repast, cast an antler before bounding away. I picked up the three-point horn and found wet blood on the 'coronet'. The deer returned to the mainland across water that whirled and bubbled with a change of tide.

The loch can rarely have been more serene than on that sunny morning when it reflected the tones and features of the upjutting hills and looked as though it had been painted. Passing gulls could admire their reflections.

As we ventured farther, I saw that the northern shore had put out a low promontory as though to tickle the cliffs on the southern side. The remaining gap was the channel into the broader reaches of Loch Hourn and we christened it the Jaws of Hell, because here was a fierce tidal rip that plucked at the boat's rudder. With four bulky men in a 14-foot boat, I half expected the craft to grate on rock or the outboard engine to prove of insufficient power to keep us on course, but all went well.

'Nae problem,' said George. Soon he had brought the boat to rest on a shell-sand beach in Barrisdale Bay.

The big hoose was there, and with it a garden behind a deer-proof fence. We admired the blooms. I glanced at my watch noted it was almost noon and told George that two friends were to be married in a few moments. I had promised to think about them as the clock reached 12. He beckoned to me, then pointed at the label on a newly-planted rose. The variety was called 'Wedding Day'.

We chatted to the wife of an estate worker whose children attended school at Inverness—as boarders, of course. Prior to this, they had been taken twice-daily across the loch, to and from Arnisdale, to attend school at Glenelg.

George lured us to the middle ground. Having walked round the bay, we journeyed to within sight of the dark cliffs of Ladhar Bheinn, which loomed beyond a small glen like the turreted walls of a medieval castle—and, it seemed to me, as impregnable. John had been reading about the Beast of Barrisdale, which has three legs, two to the fore and one aft, and is reputed to have its den in the Knoydart Hills. In the uncomfortably high temperature of a spring day, John stripped to his binoculars and boots and went bounding down the hillside! He was promptly nicknamed the Beast!

Fred and John lay in the sun, by the burn, and pronounced they did not intend to go a yard farther. George gave a Highland type of whoop and set off up the glen. Inexplicably, I went after him. I regretted it the moment we reached the bealach (pass), where the ground was so wet we used up much of our remaining energy removing our feet from the holes made as we sank into the spongy· hillside.

The crags of Ladhar Bheinn echoed to the fluty calls of cock ring ouzels. After the bogs and the bealach—or what George called 'Gaelic with Groans'—we reached the skyline, expecting to walk on to the summit of the hill. Instead, we encountered a series of formidable downs and ups—down a few hundred feet, up a few hundred feet—before we attained the highest ridge, with its snow cornice and an Ordnance Survey triangulation point. Resting on the column was a bar of Windermere butter fudge!

The sun was already well down in the western sky. We had little time to spare for the view, which included Loch Hourn, the Jaws of Hell and Heron Island. We jog-trotted towards the boat in Barrisdale Bay. At the flatlands by the bay, there remained a three-mile walk.

Fred and John were lying beside a boulder, with coats drawn over their chilling bodies; they were like Bedouins in some desert location. George, giving a Gaelic cry, leapt into the edge of the loch to cool his feet—and regretted it minutes later, as the first long shiver passed through his body.

The sun had set; the afterglow had dispersed. There remained the faint, cold light of the stars to illuminate our way back up the loch. George somehow managed not to be confused when the reflections of the hills in the water made it difficult to see just where the land ended and the water began. We felt the tug of the tidal rip against the rudder; we somehow managed to avoid protruding rocks and the islands where, the pair of herons must now be sound asleep.

Someone showed a light at Kinloch Hourn; it destroyed our 'night vision'; so that we were taken by surprise when the boat eventually rasped on the shingle. Someone staggered up the beach, found the Land-Rover, switched on the lights and enabled us to haul the boat from the water. It was 11 p.m. and we had invited some local people in for an evening meal!

We rested up next day. It gave George an opportunity to cook the haggis. He admitted his national dish was somewhat dry. 'When you eat haggis, you should have the door open to the nearest burn—or a bottle of whisky!' John went fishing and found the half-starved local trout as voracious as usual. We discovered a place where it was possible to appreciate the clarity of a burn by peering at it horizontally from the top of a waterfall: an astonishing view of what looked like a succession of subterranean caverns.

We climbed a hill, selecting Sgurr Dubh as a vantage point for the district. The sunlight strengthened and the rocks gleamed and glistened as fragments of mica caught the light head on. Large pieces of mica gleamed with a mirror-like radiance, and it seemed that dozens of heliographs were flashing out messages of greeting.

We settled down to eat, our bodies couched by warm rock. Our talk was interrupted by the farmyardy calling of greylags and 58 birds swept low over the hill, their underparts lit by the sun, revealing the fine-feather detail.

One great adventure remained—to sail to the mouth of the loch. It was a windless Easter and when, in due course, our cockleshell entered the Sound of Sleat, with Skye looking clear and cool ahead, we felt elated. What matter if the engine stopped several times on the way back to the bothy? We saw seals on obscure rocks; we spent an hour or two in the 'Ring of Bright Water' country, where Gavin Maxwell's otters had frolicked along the beach and at the waterfalls of Lower Sandaig.

As West Yorkshiremen, we felt at home in this Norse country with its main placenames incorporating 'dale' for valley. No Viking longboat sailed up Loch Hourn more proudly than did our small craft on that last voyage The boat grounded on the shore, was hauled out and the plug removed so that she would drain thoroughly.

Said George as we re-entered Perthshire: 'Nae problems.'

10 TOMORROW WON'T BE LONG
Lewis and Harris

The lady at the guest-house overlooking Uig, in northern Skye, apologised for the loud rasping sound from a nearby field. 'It's a corncrake. I hope it doesn't keep you awake.' In the early morning, unable to sleep for the monotonous double-note call, I opened the bedroom window and tried to fix the position of the bird. A huge moon was suspended over the cliffs across the Bay. The love-lorn corncrake had shifted its position from the field to the mini-jungle of the vegetable plot.

As the eastern sky greyed, the corncrake's aria had a 'backing' provided by the herring gulls assembled at the harbour to await the first holidaymakers of the day. Cars were mustering for the morning ferry to Harris. What remained of yesterday's sandwiches were thrown at the gulls.

Bird-watchers arrived. They hoped for 95 species and had already got 50 in a two-hour scrutiny of land and sky. With a considerable excess of nervous energy, they scanned the harbour and the loch with telescopes and chanted the names of birds with all the gravity of words in a litany.

Our ferry, *The Hebridean Isles*, swept in with all the pride attained by being built in Yorkshire. One of the bystanders, a Scotsman, had visited his son in Hull and returned home via Selby; he had been surprised to see the distinctive funnel of Caledonian MacBrayne above a huddle of buildings by the Ouse. The ferryboat was launched broadside on into the river.

I joined a knot of bird-watchers on the upper deck. When they had seen puffin, shag and eider, two of them slipped off to the cafeteria for bacon butties. Red-breasted merganser, cormorant, red-throated diver—we sought the refreshment area for cups of coffee and to get the chill out of our joints.

The ferry left Skye within easy viewing range of greater black-backed gull, kittiwake, herring gull, razorbill and bridled guillemot. In the Minch, a few gannets were diving, the white bodies hitting the sea with an impact that sent plumes of spray high into the air. A fulmar surveyed us with its cold Arctic eyes. Terns that had wintered in Antarctica passed us with grating calls.

I began to make notes of the passing birds, Five puffins— left to right. Fulmar—wave-skimming, right to left. Manx shearwaters—stimulated into flight by the approach of the boat, the feet of the birds pattering on the water before their long wings got sufficient lift from the waves.

As the ferry glided into Lochmaddy on North Uist, there was time to count the greater black-backed gulls nesting among tufts of sea pinks; to notice the greylag on the water and the red-throated diver setting a course for one of the hill lochans, having doubtless been feeding in the sea.

On the last stretch, to Harris, we had yet another snack in the cafeteria. I continued my bird-watching, which became difficult as windows were obscured by latecomers. I focused the binoculars on a distant window and the grey sea. Into view came a large dorsal fin. Jaws! 'There's a shark off the port bow,' I said. No one took me seriously. The steward asked, 'What's a dorsal fin?'

Then our attention was claimed by a man on the deck. He excitedly waved his arms, indicating we should join him. Was there a man overboard? Or had an albatross alighted on the ship's rail? Now he made undulating motions with his arms.

We hurried to join him and shared his elation as porpoise appeared, leaping, turning, splashing, submerging, leaping... the light bringing a gleam to their wet bodies. More porpoise passed between the ferry and shore. A basking shark is often seen at a time when porpoise are active, so presumably the dorsal fin I had reported belonged to one of the gentle giants of the sea.

Lewis and Harris were, we discovered, two names for one island. The divisions are the natural barriers of hill ranges and sea lochs. When we motored north of Tarbert, many roads had scarcely outgrown their status of tracks.

At Tarbert, we had a spell of head-scratching over the Gaelic road signs and then found the old English versions in the grounds of the Harris Hotel. George drove across the island of Harris to take possession of our bungalow on the western shore. The weather brightened a little. Ron said, 'It's almost sunny.' The hinterland of Harris would have been drab but for the many lochans reflecting the sky's various shades of grey.

The road left the area of hard rock and peaty hollows. At sea level, clean-looking sheep occupied grassy fields and the expansive sands were the feeding grounds of podgy shelduck.

Espying a telephone box, Fred decided to ring up the owner of the bungalow, to inquire where it might be found. A man's voice instructed him to look back down the road. 'You see that bungalow on the left? Well...' Our destination was in view. The womenfolk were there to greet us.

The bungalow stood on the machair—the special grassland that forms on the shell-sand beaches of some Hebridean islands and represents the best of the local grazing. In these days, much of the delicate machair is being riven about by machines and by over-grazing.

It's a Long Way to Muckle Flugga

The bungalow was protected from the sheep by a wire fence, on our side, the grass was ankle-deep; on the sheep side, it had been mown by their busy teeth until it resembled a billiards table. A wrecked caravan had been taken over by a ragged tom cat. Wheatears chacked and whistled. The dunes heaved with rabbits and beyond the dunes an azure sea broke with creamy spray on a white beach.

Watching the sheep was an introduction to 'A' level biology. It was lambing time. Whenever I looked out of a window, either casually when in the lounge or from boredom, when washing up in the kitchen, I would see yet another birth. The wee lamb was soon on its feet, being licked over by the parent ewe and receiving milk with such rapture that it nearly wagged off its tail.

Other familiar creatures were about: a black-headed gull that was lame in one foot, some common gulls and, when bread scraps were being hurled, half a dozen house sparrows. The commonest and most industrious bird on the island appeared to be the starling.

Everywhere we saw sheep. The dominant calls on Harris were the contralto bleating of ewes and the soprano arias of lambs. The shepherds of the east strode the machair with dogs at foot. Shepherds on the rocky west leaped from boulder to boulder and the dogs covered twice as much ground as they ran round the rocks and avoided the most draggly areas of ling.

During our first tour of Harris, Fred remarked on the ancient metamorphic rock. He was right. The oldest visible rocks in Europe are not at the heart of the Continent—where you have those showy upstarts, the Alps—but at the rim. Much of the Western Isles, from Lewis to Barra, consists of archaean gneiss. Where it does not reveal itself as weary-looking hills, it is yards deep in peat or covered by brackish water.

It is reckoned that 25 per cent of the land surface of the

Outer Hebrides is covered by lochans, and I can believe it, having once looked down on it from an aircraft which was beginning its slow descent to Glasgow. The sunlight brought a responsive gleam from hundreds of sheets of water.

Not surprisingly, the people live mainly at the periphery, between the moors and the sea, where land has been won by dint of hard labour over many centuries and the fields are generally the size of a few pocket handkerchiefs. The folk on the western side may be favoured by shell-sand beach and machair; those on the east have a direct view of the Minch and derive a living more from fishing than farming, with the womenfolk having a busy round that includes the weaving of Harris tweed.

Ron said the only historical personage, connected with Lewis and Harris, whom he could recall, was a Lancashire lad named Lever; and he owned the island well within living memory.

William Lever, having made a bob or two manufacturing soap, and having founded Port Sunlight near Birkenhead, became the owner of Lewis (1918) and Harris (1919). Lord Leverhulme, as he had become, may have thought he was escaping the limelight when he settled at the periphery of Britain, beside the wild Atlantic. He tried to impress his distinctive personality and ideas upon a community that was largely governed by tradition, though a number of people who had left the islands on war service returned restlessly to blackhouse and unviable croft, with the feeling that some changes might be desirable.

The English gentlemen of the nineteenth century—the new rich of the Industrial Revolution—had already made a mark, buying up land for sporting purposes, lavishing large sums of money on grandiose building schemes, decking their halls with stag heads and tartan linoleum and yet visiting their Scottish possessions for just a few weeks in the year.

During our visits to Rum we had seen how the Bulloughs of Accrington had spent liberally in building up a sporting estate that included a castle made of stone imported from Arran, a wood planted on imported soil—and a laundry set discreetly on a distant, well-hidden beach.

Lord Leverhulme was a native of Bolton who, after a lifetime of making 'brass' and building up a soap empire valued at £45 million, had no interest in retirement as such and had no inclination to don tweeds and exterminate the native birds and beasts. He had the Nonconformist work ethic. The Devil has work for idle hands! With astonishing clarity for an off-comer, he saw the major social and industrial needs of the outer islands. He devoted the last seven years of his life to island enterprises. Although he failed, he is remembered, and not without some affection, through a Gaelic name which can be translated as 'the old soap man'.

This breezy Lancastrian did not believe in outward show: he lived austerely in the castle at Stornoway, sleeping in an attic rather than in a principal bedroom. He favoured developing the island fishing industry, and especially the herring fishery which operated on the wasteful natural system of glut and scarcity. The answer, said Leverhulme, was to conserve herring in time of glut, and this he proposed to do by canning or freezing. He proposed to build a large canning factory. He foresaw a time when the marketing of fish would be done through Fleetwood, in Lancashire, the fish caught by the islanders being transported thence in refrigerated ships.

Leverhulme attempted to popularise frozen herring by having it served for breakfast at the big hoose. He had the flesh of dogfish made into fish cakes; from offal he would produce fish-meal and fertiliser; fish bones would be crushed and processed into glue. In a particularly enlightened moment he foresaw the islanders operating with large trawlers, being directed to the shoals of fish by a spotter plane.

The wreck of Leverhulme's dream came about through a number of complex issues, notably land reform, which had become a major political issue. He also encountered the opposition of crofters who were not prepared to abandon their traditional way of life, which involved crofting and inshore fishing. Eventually he sailed away from Lewis, never to return—though he did not go far, turning up on Harris where, his enthusiasm regained, he began the development of the fishing village of Obbe, re-named Leverburgh. He spent £250,000 in developing Leverburgh, building piers, kippering sheds and good homes for his employees. The house built for his own use had a tall garden wall to cheat the gales.

Leverhulme died, unexpectedly, in 1925. His executors sold off Leverburgh to a demolition company for £5,000.

We repaired on that first evening to the Harris Hotel at Tarbert, enjoying the luxuriance of its garden, where sycamores and rowan broke the monotony of treeless areas or scrubland with birch. Our meal consisted of a starter followed by beef, with boiled onions and cream sauce. Fred would have given it full marks if there had been Drambuie flavoured butter!

We awoke next day to the ringing calls of oystercatchers from the machair. The wind had a cutting edge to it. Our wee lambs had found cavities in the dunes where they could escape from being chilled through.

George took us northwards—to Lewis. Our first walk was to the head of Seaforth Loch, seeing birds everywhere on the wasteland of heather and rock—snipe, sandpiper, golden plover and a raven dressed in undertaker-black. Scores of wheatears seemed determined to invest some life into this dark countryside; they entertained us with their creaky calls and errand-boy style whistling. A. cuckoo sounded its double notes and prompted the superstitious to turn over the money in their pockets.

The name Lewis is derived from a term for flatlands. There

were green fields in the kindlier areas, away from the bluster of Atlantic gales. The vast and almost featureless landscape lay under the blue arc of the springtime sky. Where there was no land, the light had a responsive gleam from lochans that contribute to the feeling of wide open spaces. A sufferer from agoraphobia would have been in terror. Cumulus clouds drifted across a blue sky like giant wool-sacks; there was far more drama in the sky than in the landscape, yet each complemented the other. The roads were truly open. As we followed them, we felt insignificant: ant-like.

We entered the wide-flung settlement of Callanish to see the standing stones. Incredibly tall and compelling, they were formed of a type of schist called hornblende and resembled through their markings some large pieces of driftwood. I expected the stones to occupy a prominent position on the flatlands—to be visible from a great distance. Having entered the scattered settlement of Callanish, I looked feverishly around. The last feature on which my eyes rested was a hillock. It was bristling with stones. Soon I was walking in what looked like a petrified forest, with stones rising to 16 feet.

They had the sea's gleam upon them. They testified to the faith of a people who lived some 4,000 years ago. In those days, Lewis was less dreich (dreary) than it is today: the landscape was quite well wooded, the climate equable. What happened later to change the appearance of the Island—and to preserve the stones—was the onset of a wetter spell leading to the formation of up to five feet of peat. This peat lagged the stones. What protruded did not seem particularly important. When the workers of the Lewis Estate were set to work to clear the peat, one of the finest of our ancient stone assemblies was revealed virtually in mint condition.

Lewis resounds with Norse placenames—Arnol and Bragar, Carloway, Brue and Barvas. We arrived at Stornoway on the Sabbath, when scarcely anything stirred. The powerful fishing boats swung at their moorings in a fine natural harbour where once there was a fleet of 1,000 herring wherries. In those days, prior to 1914, the population of Stornoway, the only town in the Western Isles, was 4,000.

Ron, a great map-reader, showed us where the Eye Peninsula sticks out from Lewis like a thumb; he suggested a visit and soon we were standing near the lighthouse, with 60 greater black-backed gulls rising on the updraught and a blizzard of yelling kittiwakes rousing every echo. Forty miles away, visible as a smudge on the horizon, was the mainland of Scotland. A few miles farther north from where we were standing lay the Butt of Lewis, familiar to us all through daily weather broadcasts.

Men from the most northerly parish of Ness were the indomitable boatmen who for centuries sailed 40 miles through Atlantic wastes to visit the specks of land called North Rona and Sula Sgeir, the latter meaning 'gannet rock'. The main voyage, in an open boat with six oars, was to Sula Sgeir at the time of the Guga Hunt, a guga being a young gannet. In a swell or among foam-flecked waves, the men looked for a sea-rock some half a mile long and 200 yards wide at the widest place. The tradition of collecting young gannets continues, the old custom being allowed by a special provision in the Wild Birds Protection Act, 1954.

Back at the bungalow on Harris, our lives were fitted into a routine. The roof-hopping oystercatcher was our early-morning alarm. We were served with porridge made thick enough to 'point' masonry. 'Very good stuff,' said Fred as he dumped some leftover porridge in the dustbin. It was good, prepared by me and given the personal attention of George who usually pronounced it 'nae bad.' Bacon butties and good strong tea completed the meal. Any surplus bacon was made into yet more butties for the mid-day snack. Ron and Fred based their breakfast on cereals and fruit.

At Tarbert, Fred planned to walk across Harris from coast to coast. He reckoned the distance to be about 600 yards. So, starting (and ending) near the Harris Hotel he bestrode the isthmus, in an area where Lord Leverhulme planned to capitalise on the differing heights of the tides by cutting through the sliver of land and establishing a hydro-electric scheme.

George announced we would explore North Harris—that is, the part that looks as though it should be southwest Lewis—and we travelled westwards on the narrowing road to Hushinish. We found ourselves in a true Gaelic area, with names the non-Gaelic speaker might crack his false teeth on. Do your best with Sron Scourst and Amhuinnsuidhe. A native of the latter said: 'Avin-suey'.

We passed a castle and row of cannon and motored into a Scotch mist. When it thinned, a lochan was in view and on it a pair of black-throated divers. Naturally, George stopped the car. The windows were lowered as we took in the welcome sight. 'Can ye no hear the birds?' asked Fred in pidgin Scots. We listened, only to discover the sound was being made by the fan belt on George's car. 'Och, I must put some French chalk on it,' said George.

We photographed the post office at Amhuinnsuidhe a structure of corrugated iron, painted pink. The capacious postbox was brown. A buzzard swept across the moor with several angry peewits around it. The hawk, in alighting on a boulder, violated another nesting territory and was harassed yet again. The road ended with a concrete landing. place overlooking the island of Scarp. We saw a hen-hut that would not be overturned by the Atlantic gales being built of breeze-blocks and pebbledashed!

Something of the wildness went from North Harris with hydro-electrification. We had our snack meal beside a lochan where anglers were warned not to walk with their rods held upwards, in case these connected with the overhead wires. A track led us to a dam and from here we reached a lochan at an elevation of about 800 feet. On the way we were scrutinised by a golden eagle which, viewed from a pony track, was at first black against the sky and then scarcely to be seen as it moved against the dun colours of the hill.

A Lancashire lass, one of a coach party we met at the hotel, had been busy that day and rapturously described her visit to a Teddy Bear factory.

For our walk down the west coast of Harris, sunlight imparted light and warmth. We could scarcely think of ourselves as being on an oceanic island. At Leverburgh, the clarity of the light and the modest scale of the building, the smooth hills and the sparkling sea, reminded me of a visit to Iceland. At close range, we saw dereliction, where his Lordship's special enterprise had come to nought.

The common plant of wet places—yellow iris—was sending up spears of fresh green. A black guillemot floated by, enjoying the peace, and with its mate would lay eggs in a rock crevice, whereas its cousin, the common guillemot, would need the stimulation of a large cliffside colony to bring it into full breeding condition.

At the linear village of Strond, a name meaning 'strand', we heard of the recent visit of the Prince of Wales to Berneray, where he had planted tatties and enjoyed life away from the limelight. One night there had been a ceilidh. Said I, 'He'd enjoy getting away from civilisation,' and the man with whom I chatted, the local storekeeper, replied, 'He had come back to civilisation!'

I entered the store, having seen the name set on the gable end in shells. It marked out the owner as someone rather special. 'Everyone speaks Gaelic here,' he said. 'I'm speaking a foreign language now.' Fred asked him what supports the people of the Outer Isles. He pointed upwards and replied, simply, without embarrassment, 'The Lord above. He will supply all your needs. We have a marvellous way of life up here.'

He had been brought up in a blackhouse, the simple stone-walled, thatched hoose of rural Scotland. His home had 'originally' been thatched, but during his early life the thatch was replaced by felt, then by corrugated asbestos, then slate. It was now simply a ruin!

With typical island hospitality, he invited us to his bungalow home overlooking the sound and the skerries. In the clearest weather, he said, St. Kilda might be seen 50 miles away. That lonely archipelago is in the parish of Harris. We were shown frescoes and ornamental pieces, formed of oddments set in concrete. Much had been picked up on the shore. One surprising item that found a place in the scheme was a telegraph insulator! Then he pointed out new uses for old telephone kiosks. One was being used by a crofter as a small greenhouse and he had a panel from another kiosk. set in the front door of his shop. Its weight ensured that it would not be blown off its hinges.

He directed us to a path leading through some sweet limestone country to the south-eastern tip of Harris. As usual, each view was backed by a vista of the gleaming sea. In easy stages we came to the church of St Clement at Rodel, which was built in about 1500 on the cruciform plan, a novelty m the Outer Isles. We who had been walking near outcrops of pearl-grey limestone now had the novelty of being in a building where mellow green sandstone some of it imported from Mull, lay about us.

There remained a steady walk back to Leverburgh, which until the off-comer Lord's day had been known as Obbe. Lord Leverhulme chose it for development because it might have become a base for fishing boats and was equally handy for the Atlantic and the Minch.

Our afternoon was spent on the machair of the north-west—at the Toe Head of Harris. We crossed many acres of fine, stable grassland which now was alive with waders including dunlin in their breeding garb. The grassland once nurtured many cattle and is now used mainly for sheep.

The sun brought out the fresh greenness of the sward—a tract of land on which none of the modern artificial fertilisers had been used, with the result that in late spring and summer it is a carpet of flowers. Beyond the machair was sun-bleached sand, culminating in the far distance with the azure sea and the blue hills of North Harris.

The beach had an eye-searing whiteness. We reached the ruins of a small chapel decorated by sea pinks that were in full bloom. Beef cattle lay nearby, reminding us of the former huge trade in Island stock bought by mainland dealers.

While George gallantly agreed to drive the car round to Borve, we three followed the way of the sands. At the lower end of the machair, a lapwing chick ran briskly on stilt-like legs and then dropped near a tussock and became immobile. The medley of the machair was rich and diverse. Dunlin uttered their shimmering trills; the sound seemed to hang in the still air. Wheatears wheezed and whistled near the rabbit holes, golden plover piped as they ran with mincing steps, and the sheep and lambs ensured that it was never absolutely quiet.

When the Hebridean Sahara ended, the voices of common gulls could be heard from their colony on the low grassland. Some adventurous birds had their nests on isolated dunes away from the main shoreline. One pair had simply deposited eggs in a scrape without a scrap of nesting material, which was just as well or the nest would have been seen by predators...

George had originally intended us to stay on the Isle of Scalpay. He had heard of an old lighthouse where paying guests were welcome. He mentioned that where the road ran out, it was necessary to walk across half a mile of moor. We had decided against that exciting venture, but at least we arranged to set aside a day to visit the lighthouse. Scalpay was revealed as a well-populated, proud little island.

The people were still using some of the old lazybeds either for the growing of potatoes or, if sufficiently peaty, aa fuel for their fires. As we left the ferry, free-range hens were having a dust bath—repeat, dust bath—beside the single road.

Fishing boats were being repainted near the rusting remains of a pre-1914 steam drifter. A wren sang from a mooring rope and a whinchat used a telegraph pole as a song perch. One of the island collies adopted us for a mile or two. The Islanders were fond of tethering animals. We saw a tethered calf, a tethered tup and a tethered lamb, presumably an orphan.

The hard road ended half a mile from the lighthouse on Eilean Glas. There followed a turbary (peat-cutter's) way. Husband and wife teams were scattered about the dark brown face of the moor. Two peat-diggers were cleaning their tuskas (spades). The inhabitants of the island, known as Scalpachs, form a splendidly independent fellowship with a regard for their environment.

The island postman passed and we watched his slow progress to the lighthouse, across the moor, using a route indicated by yellow markers. I followed him. A Great Dane with arthritic hind legs and a mournful howl in turn followed me to the buildings where coffee was on sale at a holiday centre that appeals to many for its remoteness and novel setting. The lighthouse, dating from 1788, was the first to be built on the Western Isles. A plaque commemorates the demise of one of the last of the great auks. I was reminded by the new owner of the buildings that Gavin Maxwell had his shark-hunting enterprise, about which he wrote in a still readable book, on this island of Scalpay.

We had walked into a north-west wind, which brought colour to our cheeks and sharpened our appetites. Our evening meal at Tarbert was venison, neaps (turnip) and tatties (potatoes). Fred looked as pleased as the Scalpach who had been sitting in the sunshine when other islanders had scurried about, handling the peats. As we passed, this man had remarked: 'I've got an all electric home.'

Next day, we again ventured along the road to Scalpay, but this time it was our intention to visit Rhenigidale, a remote community approached on a route said to be comparable with some in the Andes. We were caught up in traffic for the Scalpay ferry and we shared the general annoyance when a man with a JCB decided to dig up a strip of road so that a pipe could be laid. 'Och,' he said to an inquirer, 'tomorrow won't be long.' He softened the conversation by telling about the wee lassie who was asked to spell 'loch' and replied: 'Ell Oh Ock Ock.' We laughed loudly and long—and then wondered why!

The queue of traffic consisted of a large delivery van, an ambulance, a red car, a Council van and the mobile library. The ambulance was on its way to collect an old lady for treatment. The car belonged to a lively 90-year-old hotelier. In due course, the pipe was put in place, the trench filled in with loose material and the traffic moved again. As we crossed the trench, there was a tooth-shifting jolt.

We began to walk along a grassy track to an elevation of 970 feet. The gradient was comfortable in a landscape which George pronounced 'dreich'. In due course, a cairn was reached. The Shiant Islands—the name means 'enchanted'— had their hard outlines softened by distance. No one lives on the Shiants today. The islanders of old hunted seabirds on the cliffs of Garbh Eilean.

Our Andean experience was a descent of 1,000 feet, in a dozen mighty zig-zags, on a green track polished by the postman's boots. He uses it three times a week—a total of 6,000 feet. As we descended, a wren was in glorious song. Ferns were unfolding and had reached the stage where they resembled bishops' croziers. The coastline—its rocks, skerries and islands— assumed various pastel shades, set against a shimmering sea.

The path contoured on the cliffs. We passed the remains of a settlement where sheep were now the caretakers and spring flowers bloomed, among them tormentil and butterwort.

Rhenigidale, five miles from where we had left the car remained out of sight until we were almost upon it. I was amazed at the density of golden plover on the hills round about. They greatly outnumbered the eleven people. I heard of two children attending a school that was walled and roofed with corrugated iron. A hostel, owned by the Gatcliffe Trust, had by a curious chance eleven beds. I chatted to the lady who had been warden for 25 years.

For the return, George went ahead. At the watershed, he left some messages scrawled in peaty pools with the point of his walking stick. The first announced: 'George—Gone on!' We walked a few yards to the second message: 'Magic! It's downhill!'

Back at the bothy, the local farmers had organised a round-up of sheep and lambs. Half a dozen men and as many dogs appeared. The sheep moved in bleating throngs to the pens where they would be sorted. Some of the ewes energised by panic, scrambled over a dyke onto the road and the dogs were bidden to round them up.

Early next morning, the machair was almost empty. As sunlight banded the dewy ground with yellow, cramped sheep stood up and lambs bleated to keep up their spirits. It was time to leave Harris. The ferry bore us back across the Minch to Uig, from where we followed roads southwards through Skye, with gentle hills, woods, well-kept crofts and larches bright with new foliage, offering a contrast with the Outer Isles.

At the Narrows, two golden eagles were working the face of a moor together, when the local hooded crows would allow them. The eagles seemed ponderous against the much smaller, dapper crows. This battle of wits and patience—this harrying of the eagles by the crows and the evasive action—went on for perhaps 20 minutes and was still in progress as we moved off.

'When I first saw those eagles through binoculars,' said Fred, 'I thought two helicopters were approaching!'

Another ferry took us across to Mallaig and soon we were at the familiar Lochailort hotel, hearing about current deer movements. Stimulated by the information that about 30 stags regularly moved from the hill to the lochside at dusk, I left the hotel with Fred and Ron to intercept the animals.

A fine stag was grazing cheekily in the garden a few yards away. The animal was in excellent condition and showing new antler growth; it would weigh around 17 stone. The woman at the house shouted; her dog barked. The stag went quietly over the fence, with great economy of effort, and had soon vanished among the trees.

George joined us. We set off deering and, in the end, enjoyed the spectacle of a Hebridean sunset, with the strongest colours behind the Cuillins of Skye: lofty, serrated, blue-black hills against the gold of a clear sky.

11 AT THE EDGE OF THE WORLD
St Kilda

St Kilditis, an incurable disease, is neither painful nor debilitating. It is characterised by a deep longing for St Kilda, that scattering of volcanic islands and stacks some 50 miles off the Western Isles. St Kilditis is alleviated by reading about them or by making the long, sometimes stormy crossing to 'the islands at the edge of the world'.

I was afflicted some 40 years ago, when I read *With Nature and a Camera*, a book written and illustrated by Richard and Cherry Kearton, grown-up men who reverted to a mental age of 11 when let loose on some remote island. They were boys at heart. Having visited St Kilda in 1896, they left a graphic account of their adventures. It began with the sea crossing:

> When we got clear of the Hebrides, and were fairly launched upon the bosom of the mighty Atlantic, the waves began to make themselves felt, and to render the after-deck uninhabitable except for such as could don oilskins... Towards noon, the weather thickened considerably, and a drizzling rain commenced to fall. The steamer was now rolling and pitching...
>
> As we passed Rock Lavenish, the ship got the full benefit of wind and tide on her port, and, in consequence, rolled fearfully. Her decks were often at such an acute angle that the sailors themselves were obliged to hold on to whatsoever stable article lay within reach.

Happily, in Village Bay, on the main island of Hirta, the water was calm, although they did hear the tide growling in the caves of Dun, which forms a natural breakwater.

On the voyage to St Kilda, the weather can be so calm that seabirds admire their reflections in the Atlantic, or so bad that even the seasickness pills turn green. I wrote to the National Trust for Scotland requesting a place on one of its summer work-parties. They put my name on the list of those going in June. All that remained was to hope for a calm sea and a pleasant voyage.

So that year while Fred, Ron and George—together with the 'lasses'—went to the glens of Perthshire, I voyaged 100 miles west of mainland Scotland. The Weather Clerk was in a benign mood. The only white water I saw was the sea-foam at the bows of *MV Monaco*, a converted trawler now concerned with cruising along the Scottish seaboard. The National Trust for Scotland were using *Monaco* to transport its work-parties. Cubby MacKinnon, the skipper, delights in the tumult of water at the bows of a sea-going ship. He derives as much pleasure from it as someone else might get from looking at the varied forms and shapes in a good coal fire. He and his wife Kate work together on *Monaco*.

My adventure began on a bonnie morning at Oban. A dozen of us, all cheerful volunteers, with Ron Hardie as the party leader, stood on a quay looking down, down, down to where *Monaco* waited at low tide.

There was work to be done—a fortnight's food supply, plus our luggage, to stow away below decks. The stock of food formed an impressive heap, for St Kilda is more than a day's sailing from the nearest supermarket. With the boat's deck far below the quay, we lowered the substantial items of food and kit by rope. Vegetables were dropped and 'fielded' by someone on deck. Holidaymakers on the quay stared open-mouthed at the spectacle of free-flying bananas and cabbages.

The eggs, in their papier-mache boxes, were passed from hand to hand. It was ironic that we should be taking eggs to St Kilda, where several million seabirds lay eggs. Years ago, the St Kildaans consumed seabirds and eggs, storing any surplus for use in the winter.

At noon, the propeller of *MV Monaco* stirred some life into the calm water of Oban Bay. The boat left a herringbone pattern on the Sound of Mull—a pattern that became complex when our wake was crossed by a MacBrayne car ferry and then by a tall-masted ship from Ireland.

Rounding Ardnamurchan, I looked eagerly for the familiar shapes of the Small Isles. I bowed gravely towards the Cuillins of Skye and winked at MacLeod's Maidens (a group of stacks). A friend of Cubby pointed to one of the last two of the diesel-powered puffers, the 'workhorses' of the Western Isles, which had just delivered a load of coal to Dunvegan and was returning to Ayr. 'Coal's cheapish just now...'

For years, my dreams had been coloured by accounts I had read of remote, little-visited St Kilda, which came into being with the flaring of a large ring volcano some 60 million years ago. The islands and stacks are what remain and they are being ceaselessly eroded by the mighty Atlantic which, in a few more million years, will have gobbled up the lot.

For centuries, the self-reliant folk of St Kilda were in part a 'bird people', relying on the nesting seafowl for food for lamp-oil and for feathers to be bartered with the Factor for necessities brought from the mainland. The traditional way of life ended when the population declined to 36 and, in August 1930, was evacuated.

St Kilda was visited by yachtsmen, by naturalists or trawlermen until, in the 1950s, a small military base was established on Hirta for monitoring the launching of rockets from Benbecula. Today the islands are owned by the National Trust for Scotland, who have leased them to the Nature Conservancy Council. They were declared a National Nature Reserve in 1957 and appear on the World Heritage List. The Ministry of Defence sub-leases a small area.

Humans are vastly outnumbered by the seals and the seabirds. Hereabouts is the world's largest gannetry and the oldest and largest colony of fulmars in Britain. Here the puffins fly like bumble bees pouring from a hive and eiders sit tightly on their nests like streaky brown puff-balls.

On that first day of voyaging from Oban to St Kilda, the sun set redly, among a mass of blue-black cloud. I had the impression that the western sky was bleeding. We reached Lochmaddy on North Uist under the binoculared gaze of an officer on the bridge of the MacBrayne car ferry—a huge vessel ablaze with electric light. Cubby made a neat job of securing *Monaco*.

For several hours we slept; the boat's engine was still. Then Cubby and Kate were up and about, the boat came back to life and I reached the deck in time to observe that magical moment at dawn when all is still. The sea was as calm as the proverbial millpond: if a jellyfish had surfaced, I would have noticed the faint ripple.

The Sound of Harris was our route to the Atlantic. We did not know what conditions to expect beyond the natural breakwater of the Western Isles, so Kate dampened the cloths on the tables of the saloon to provide extra adhesion for anything placed upon them. In the galley, the knives began to rattle, but the crossing was 'nae so bad'.

We left a clear sky and slipped under a canopy of cloud. It was not actually raining but sometimes the air had such liquid consistency it might almost be called drizzle. When St Kilda came into view, afar off, the islands wore poultices of cloud.

I had a peculiar pleasure in seeing St. Kilda as a smudge on the horizon when, for so many years, it had been familiar only through photography. The archipelago consists of four islands—Hirta, Dun, Soay and Boreray—each appearing to leap directly from the sea, such is the spectacular nature of cliffs rising to over 1,000 feet. Some of the attendant stacks were tall enough to tickle the passing clouds.

Cubby ignored our final destination, Hirta, and made directly for Boreray, four miles away, intent on showing us some big colonies of seabirds. We had the company of birds that had been feeding. They had yet to run the gauntlet of the great skuas.

Gannet, puffin, guillemot and razorbill flew purposefully, overtaking the *Monaco* with ease. Gannets rode the air currents with stiffened wings, the auks working their wings so briskly I half-expected some of them to break off. All were heading for Boreray and its stacks.

We approached a grey wall, topped by summer-green pasturage for the many sheep that were left here at the time of the evacuation and which now are the unofficial green-keepers of this uninhabited island, keeping it neat and tidy.

The *Monaco* came close to cliffs that held rows of growling gannets, some of which flew to join the traffic in a bird-busy sky. The presence of the boat did not alarm them. Years ago, a tourist spectacle was provided by the skipper of a steamer when he sounded the whistle and thousands of gannets rose simultaneously into the air.

We rounded the island and saw Stac an Armin, Britain's highest sea stack, whitened by nesting birds. We passed Stac Lee. These geological remnants rose like the fangs of some monster. Gannets, silhouetted against the sun's glare, wheeled above the rock.

The *Monaco* was now directed to Hirta; we reached Village Bay. The Keartons wrote of the 'sombre grandeur of the place'.

That was before an Army camp was constructed, and before Gemini inflatable craft with outboard motors scurried across the bay like brightly-coloured water beetles...

An Army landing craft slipped by on the high tide and allowed itself to be stranded on a crescent of fine sand until the next tide. The beach is present only in summer, for winter storms disperse the sand in deeper water. When the LCL (Landing Craft Logistics) are unable to land, the St Kilda detachment is supplied by helicopter or by Cessna aircraft.

The Cessna specialises in dropping containers with stores and mail on to a tract of flat ground on a hill overlooking Village Bay. One day a luckless soldier on the ground was injured when a bag burst and he was struck by a flying chicken. That chicken was like a missile, having been plucked and frozen!

I eagerly looked beyond the Army complex to locate the famous Street, between the old meadowland and the hill. Archaeologists have detected several phases of habitation. What remains of the small Victorian houses are the most prominent features in the Street. They were small, 'two ee's and a moo", yet, with their chimneys intact they have a dignity even in decay.

Most of the Street itself is grassed over. It was here that the St Kildan males met each workaday morning as the Parliament, discussing the tasks to be carried out that day. The Street with its sixteen houses, once held a large population. Now the area where the St Kildans lived, loved, raised children and died is patrolled by fulmars which stare at intruders unblinkingly. St Kilda wrens try to infuse a sense of life into an ancient settlement by singing at full volume.

The Street is mown daily by the Soay sheep, one of the most primitive types in Europe, which on St Kilda are virtually untouched by human hands, being allowed to live their lives without interference. The sheep also litter the Street with moulted wool, chestnut or black. The wool has moulted naturally; once it was a valuable crop, being plucked, not shorn.

I watched a researcher trailing a group and collecting fresh droppings in small glass jars for study. She had also developed the art of catching sheep at dead of night by sneaking up on the cleits, the old storage places of the St Kildans, which the animals use as dormitories.

The Soay sheep are on St Kilda by right of 1,000 generations. No one is sure how they got here, but they might have been brought by the Vikings. Unlike mainland sheep, which can be enticed by food, these Artful Dodgers would not tolerate close scrutiny. They were flighty creatures. If I stopped, they soon bounded away. The population builds up and then crashes, which is a natural way. It had recently lost about 50 per cent of its strength, but the survivors would soon restore the old numbers.

Soay sheep are spirited animals from birth. I watched two small lambs head-butting. The small black lamb gave way, turned and began to graze. The chestnut lamb ungallantly butted the other from behind. I mentioned this to a retired vet who was in our party: he smiled and forecast a bright future for the chestnut lamb!

All the masonry in the Street had been made secure by work-parties of the National Trust for Scotland; they had also roofed and refurbished five of the houses. In the first, our meals were prepared and served. We surreptitiously sprinkled a few crumbs on the floor for the St Kilda mice, which turned up at about 10 p.m.

The island sub-species of long-tailed field mouse is quite a character; it scutters about the Street in the gloaming, and by invading houses it occupies a niche once held by the St Kilda house mouse, now extinct.

It was never really dark. The Hebridean summer night is brief enough; on Hirta, the orange glare from sodium chloride at the Army base tinted the clouds, and the throbbing from the generator house provided a rhythmical background to the strident voices of oystercatchers and mingled with the voices of storm petrels coming in from the ocean to their nests in the big wall between the old Factor's House and the Feather Store.

Anyone who yearned for the noisy pleasures of civilization might go to the Puff Inn, at the Army base, an establishment described on a leaflet available locally as being famous (or infamous) for its low prices and flexible opening hours. One might drink to the accompaniment of a juke box. Everyone was friendly.

In the bar, one evening, I was shown a Union Jack shredded by a winter gale. The flag had been raised on the mast just before the gale arrived, and the force of the wind was such that no one could recover the flag for days on end. One blast of wind topped 195 miles an hour.

The commanding officer told me that Spring arrived on the first of April. That was the day when the first puffin was reported; when the first Soay lamb was seen and when it was possible to walk out and about without going ankle-deep in mud.

Many of us kept unsociable hours. A Midlander went fishing from the rocks and returned, sometimes in the wee small hours, with a score of fish. A braw Scot took his sleeping bag up the hill and slept under the stars, blithely ignoring warnings about sheep ticks and 'keds'. My chief nocturnal pleasure apart from sleeping was visiting the wall where the storm petrels nested, listening to the guttural voices of the birds and occasionally seeing bat-like forms in the sky as the time for a change-over in nesting duties arrived.

The Hebridean night was vibrant with the 'bleating' of snipe which went into shallow glides, extending the outer feathers of their tails so that the wind passed through the stiffened barbs, with a wavering sound. Snipe were common nesters around the village.

Walking could be combined with bonxie-dodging. Wherever I went—through the Gap to the cliffscape between Conachair and Oiseval, or along the western rim to the Cambir, or even to the western limit of Village Bay, at Ruaival—great skuas made the air crackle with their guttural voices. They were nesting on the drier parts of the hills. Off-duty birds perched on knolls and tussocks. The voice of the skua—'keg, keg'—punctuated my excursions as birds wheeled, taking the upthrust of the breeze on wings with an impressive span, some four-and-a-half feet. The skua weighs over three pounds and is therefore among the avian heavyweights.

No self-respecting bonxie fears a human intruder into its territory. If I had not taken note of the calls, then I could not ignore the dive, with the hefty bird passing my head at a range of a few inches. The first bird to dive on me used guile as well as physical strength, tending to fly towards me from the rear. A sudden 'whoosh' of displaced air was followed by another round of cackling.

Skuas usually nest in treeless northern places where there is no possibility of securing a stick to hold above the head as a deterrent. I was on Hirta at the time when eggs were hatching. Now and again I came across a downy youngster, waddling on webbed feet that seemed a few sizes too large for the bird!

Great skuas were the guardians of the Tunnel, a natural rock arch on the northern shore. As I slithered down the hill towards it, the large brown birds lumbered into flight and then let the rising air carry them aloft. I was also entertained to the air display of the fulmar petrels; the birds disappeared and reappeared at the edge of a cliffs and made dramatic movements of wings and tail feathers to maintain their equilibrium in a fierce updraught.

The Army provided a Gemini inflatable to convey us across the Bay for a landing on Dun, the jagged outline of which had become a familiar feature during our stay in the village. An eider duck cruised by with a duckling on its back. Rafts of puffins in the Bay testified to the high population on Dun. We landed to the croaking of fulmars, which had settled on every suitable cliffscape, high or low.

Dun is dominated by birds and the sea. Every niche on the long narrow ridge was being used for nesting. The sharp crest of the island gave it a special character, dividing the southern side—where the cliffs were up to 500 feet high—from the northern, where steeply shelving slopes were riddled with puffin burrows.

Kittiwakes had plastered their nests against the merest knobs of rock in a shallow cave. Razorbills, immaculate, clad in black and white, like birds in a dress suit, did not seem to mind being peered at from close range. Puffins alighted with glistening sand-eels in their beaks, testifying to the presence of young in the peaty burrows.

We had work to do, of course. One group completed the re-roofing of the first house in the Street; another had some joinery projects; a third was concerned with the renovation of cleits. Each cleit was numbered. I became a member of the 123 Club when I visited Cleit 122 and crawled along a tunnel into the beehive-shaped Cleit 123. Our veterinary friend, emerging slowly from the tunnel which he virtually filled, used his vet's knowledge to extricate himself. 'The first principle of calving,' he announced, 'is to get one shoulder through first.'

Then we thought of home. One of our party made a 'St Kilda mail-boat'—a small, boat-shaped piece of wood, hollowed to accommodate mail and capable of being sealed to make it watertight, attached to a buoyant object. Years ago, an animal bladder was used; we found a plastic container.

When the boat had received its items of mail and had been sealed, it was taken to the Point, to be placed on the ebb tide and, hopefully, to make good progress across to the Western Isles, where it would be picked up and the contents posted to our homes.

The boat was released on the evening of June 16. The postcard I had placed in it was delivered to my home in Giggleswick, Yorkshire, on June 27.

On my return home I gazed at the picture on the card. It had been taken from Hirta, looking across four miles of sea to Boreray and the stacks. The main island was poulticed by cloud. It did not need much effort to imagine the gannets plunge-diving in the sea and to hear the croaking of many fulmars.

I was beginning to get more pangs of St Kilditis. I must return before long to 'the islands at the edge of the world'.

12 SORTIES IN SUTHERLAND
Inchnadamph and Durness

North of the Great Glen we stopped for a meal at a large log cabin in which fragrant (choking) smoke wafted across the room from an open fire. 'They're kippering us,' said Fred.

A notice on Struie Hill mentioned 'No Sunday Gritting'. We stopped, shivering, and looked deep into Sutherland—to Ben Klibreck (28 miles) and Ben More Assynt (30 miles). As we drove northwards from Bonarbridge, George discovered he had left his sleeping bag at home.

The deer kept to the skyline and the sheep were monarchs of the glens—big, clean-looking Cheviot sheep, not yet with lambs at foot, for it was early April. Sheep not only dominated the landscape but thronged the roads. George drove safely through a flock of about 150 sheep that had four barking dogs and three shouting men in attendance. Fred's car almost disappeared from sight behind a mass of woolly bodies.

The sun gained mastery of the sky and the heat cleared away the last tatters of cloud. The clarity of the air was such that everything stood out in fine detail. We beheld Beinn Stack, which by its shape might be Sheihallion's northern cousin. Ben Arkle's great ridge was layered with snow. The lochans looked so blue they might have been filled with ink.

We marvelled at the stylish use of concrete forms on the bridge at Kylesku, which replaced a free ferry. Ron, Fred and lots of other Yorkshiremen would journey hundreds of miles into this part of Scotland—simply to use the free ferry!

Inchnadamph was 430 miles from home, but we felt at home because of the limestone escarpment. The Scottish elements in the landscape included a large loch, an islanded castle, a big hoose, a big hotel, a home for the shepherd and his family—and our wee bothy, to which we were greeted by a fluffy cat, half Persian. The cat let out two friendly yowls, arched its back and rubbed itself against the garden gate. Two hens were pecking at the body of a late relative—slain under the speeding wheels of a lorry. It seemed a pity that the hen, having survived the long, hard northern winter, had not managed to stay alive long enough to enjoy the spring.

As bothies go, the one at Inchnadamph was fine—stout, of simple construction, with a slate roof. Inside was a living room, a kitchen, two bedrooms and a bathroom. The fire roared against a back boiler and heated the system so efficiently that when someone had a bath and turned on the hot tap there was a dramatic mixture of hot water and steam, which rolled through the place like fog on the Newfoundland Banks. We 'mashed' some tea, which, when poured, was 'hot as hell and black as t'fireback'.

As the sun reached the western bens, we walked to the hotel and joined the anglers and geologists in the dining room. On our return, peewits were calling from the flats, and the thin air seemed to vibrate to the 'bleating' of snipe. George had invited some of the lads for a tipple. One of our guests said, 'Nice wee corner, this.' Another advised us to' 'get that coal right up that chimney; you'll need the heat.' Fred was convinced that when anyone opened a bottle of whisky, subtle signals were transmitted up to three miles away.

A tall lad drank a quarter of a bottle without water and continued to speak lucidly. A crofter appeared and disappeared, meanwhile becoming a little drunker than he had been on his first appearance. A dark-haired chap restricted himself to a few wee sips at a can of lager, for he had to drive 245 miles to

Glasgow—to go to work.

Sometime during the night, I awoke, shivered, crept from my bed at the far end of the house and reassembled my bedding under the table in the living room, where the embers of the big fire provided a cherry-red glow.

We left the bothy by car to pay our respects to the Old Man of Stoer, one of the big sandstone sea stacks of this part of the coast. The landscape and its wild creatures had not yet forgotten winter; a dozen hooded crows had assembled at a feeding place for sheep. The oystercatchers were still in small flocks and had not yet reached the excitable stage.

At 1 p.m. we were sitting at the cairn on Stoer Head, looking west to where the Western Isles lay under a long white cloud. Snow adorned the peaks of South Uist and Barra. Even Mingulay was in sight. Eastwards was an impressive grouping of the Sutherland bens, capped by white but otherwise dove-grey under cloud. We had walked along a coastline which became higher, grander, with every footfall until the cliffs were hundreds of feet high. The rock was dull red Torridonian sandstone and the wet ground sustained an impoverished vegetation.

We watched a ubiquitous wren dart in and out of a patch of heather on the cliff edge as a raven glided silently by, the sunlight bringing a silvery sheen to the dark feathers. Then along came a fulmar, on its stiff wings, performing graceful movements in the air through simple adjustments of its feathers and without once flapping its wings.

Our evening meal featured onion soup, duckling and apple crumble. We were also provided with a large teacake (Bap giganticus!). The manager mentioned the gilleroo, a special type of trout found in one loch. When our faces registered disbelief, he produced a specimen in a glass-fronted case. We were told to observe that there were no red spots to the sides of the body.'And the gilleroo is said to have a double stomach.' Ron wanted to know if it chewed its cud!

With Ron on scavenging duty, he vanished early and returned with some gnarled wood with which to start the fire. It was vital work. During the night, the living room temperature dropped 20 degrees. The fields were white over with hoar frost. Fred turned on the radio. The weather forecaster gave a doleful account of what had happened, adding that no icebergs had been reported 'so there are no problems on the ferries.'

Down on the flats by the loch, the lapwings were demonstrative; one produced the familiar buzzing sound with its wings as it circled in agitation. Perhaps there was a fox in the area. The post-bus arrived and we pointed to the letterbox. A mistake had been made in the spelling of the place—Inchwadamph.

Ron was anxious to visit what he called 'Kodak Country'. We could not resist extending the expedition to Ullapool, having heard of the Russian invasion. A Soviet fishing fleet layoff the coast and periodically the men slipped ashore to buy goods that were non-existent, uncommon or very costly at home. The post office was sometimes half full of Russians and queues developed at the telephone kiosks as men waited to ring up their families in Murmansk 'We call the Russians the "klondikers",' said one of the shop-owners. Amazingly, bus trips had been organised to take them to the city stores.

The principle feature of Ron's 'Kodak Country' was Stac Polly, which looked twice as high as the 2,009 feet with which it is credited. From the road to Reiff, we saw its castellated profile. We were travelling on yet another promontory; the road petered out where the sea was smacking its lips against Torridonian rock and to the south lay the Summer Isles. As we debated the origin of the name Fred murmured, 'Summer here and summer there...'

It was decided to devote the next day to a quest for the gilleroo, Sutherland's mysterious sub-species of trout. Having 'mucked out'—Fred's term for cleaning up the hoose—we began our hill walk, the sweet song of cock ring ouzels being periodically drowned by the roar of low-flying jet aircraft. A meadow pipit, much more adroit in flight, descended like a shuttlecock; buzzards were demonstrating the art of gliding, and a peregrine falcon put on a burst of avian speed near some lofty cliffs.

We reached Stevenson's 'vacant wine-red moor', visually at its least interesting until we flushed two red hinds and watched a pair of goldeneye circle a tarn with 'whickering' sound. Our arrival at the gilleroo tarn was attended by a shaft of sunlight. We walked round the tarn, waited, watched and tossed half a sandwich in the water, but it must have been siesta time for twin-stomached trout. None was seen. We collected some moulted deer hair and a grouse feather to act as 'memory hooks' of a moorland walk in Sutherland.

At the bone caves of Allt nan Uamh, George fed the ravens and eagles. He was the first to finish his snack meal, which we had by a dried-up river-bed; he followed the goat tracks up the hillside to where the limestone had been eroded, and showed not the least surprise when he found the rotting corpse of a Cheviot ewe. Declaring this to be a potential health hazard to visitors, he hurled it off the cliff where hungry birds would soon reduce it to bleached bones.

Exploring what is possibly the most northerly palaeolithic cave site in mainland Britain was a familiar experience to those of us who had visited Victoria Cave, on the limestone above Ribblesdale. Here in Sutherland, archaeologists had removed the bones of bear, reindeer, lynx and lemming. Humans were here some 8,000 years ago.

Early Man would have marvelled at the organization behind the serving of dinner at the hotel we frequented each evening.

The gong went precisely at 7 p.m. It was an immense gong, momentarily stunning the senses of anyone standing within ten yards of it. Geological students who had been jockeying for position now exploited whatever advantage they had secured and within seconds—or so it seemed—each had found a place and sat with soup spoon in hand.

George, with something of Drake's mentality, insisted on finishing his wee drammie before going into the dining room. By 7.42 p.m. precisely, the students had departed, the tables were being cleared and rearranged for breakfast and we were the only diners left. For the record, the meal was vegetable soup, braised ox tongue, and Norwegian cream cheese, with coffee to follow in the lounge.

We felt as contented as palaeolithic man must have been when his mate served up a tasty bear steak or best cut of reindeer. In the gloaming, the sky was tinted red and orange. The big hills were dark-grey and purple, their edges so well defined they might have been cardboard cut-outs. And next day we planned an outing to a special type of scenery—Sandwood Bay, a mini-Sahara by the ocean.

The weather changed during the night. I heard a loud roaring, like an express train, heralding the arrival of the local wind, which we had christened Morag. The wind blew open the front door and howled down the passage.

At daybreak, the technicoloured landscape had become grey; the big bens were wrapped in cloud and the wind was from the north. The route across the moor to Sandwood did not lack variety. We negotiated peat, boulders, and the sandy edges of lochans, all in a lack-lustre landscape of out-of-season moorland under cloud. The heather looked stunted, as though it had given up the struggle against the elements and was keeping its head down. The moorland seemed endless.

I will not claim that the weather improved at the moment Sandwood Bay came into sight. Perhaps, being sheltered from the north, this area had been bright all day. What I do remember is that the sky held individual clouds rather than one huge mass of vapour; that the wind appeared to be less cruel as I began to descend and that there was a strong impression of leaving a desert and entering an oasis.

The sea was coloured like jade, except where foam-crested waves formed as the beach shelved or there were obtrusive rocks. In the bay itself, the waves seemed to run out of energy and fall back on themselves through sheer fatigue. The beach lay between the sea and a loch, so that one stretch of water had a different hue from the other. The big, dry dunes were thatched with marram grass.

My experience of Scotland reached one of its high points as I walked on the broad beach towards the sea. Musical themes are often in mind when I am in the countryside: now I found myself recalling the crashing strains at the opening of Vaughan Williams' Sea Symphony—BEHOLD THE SEA! I imagined massed voices; massed instrumentalists and brought to mind music that seemed to fit exactly a breath-taking scene of giant waves advancing to destruction against smooth, golden sand. The water kept the lower part of the beach wet and shiny; it provided a mirror reflection of the sea, with its cushions of cumulus cloud.

BEHOLD THE SEA! Waves were breaking up on lumps of Torridonian Sandstone, draped with kelp. The gulls offshore were facing a stiff wind and so kept their wings tucked well in. To the south, providing a focal point, was a sandstone stack, Am Buachaille, against which the sea spent itself ina flurry of wind and water.

It was too much for the senses. I joined the others. With numbed mind, I sat munching sandwiches in the lee of the rocks. We kept silent vigil in that lonely bay with its flanking cliffs and a stack that had the visual emphasis of an exclamation mark.

The wind shifted. Trillions of grains of sand were blown to the dunes, continuing that subtle readjustment of the scene we call erosion. Freshwater seeped from the beach, passing through a fine filter of sand. At the loch, greater blackbacked gulls washed the salt water from their feathers and greeted us with mournful voices.

We returned to Sutherland in June. Our base, the splendidly named Far North Hotel, near Durness, had been adapted from a special wartime building and was novel indeed. The Brown family who owned it had property in the Yorkshire Dales; the wood used to make the frame of a sun lounge had been brought from Wensleydale. When I sauntered out, the outcropping limestone I passed was reminiscent of the Dales.

Yet in this far-northern landscape skuas sail-planed at the sea's edge; a corncrake's rasping voice was commonplace. Water in the bays had such clarity I watched a red-throated diver fishing beneath the surface. It was exhilarating to stride across a wide beach on which no other person had ventured since the last tide and, at Cape Wrath—the 'turning point'—to see some of the most formidable mainland cliffs in Britain.

I left the hotel, putting to flight some common gulls that had assembled on the lawn for kitchen scraps. The limestone terrain supported orchids—early purple, northern marsh and heath-spotted. I found acres of mountain avens near the sea. Also in view were water avens, bogbean, marsh marigold, mountain everlasting, twayblade, alpine bistort, fairy flax— and a host more. A ginger tom cat was stalking a starling. A sandpiper went off with rippling song and wings held stiffly out but vibrating like the prongs of a tuning fork. The rock doves I saw appeared to be the true species and not hybrids. Within five minutes walk of the hotel I was in the nesting territory of a pair of greenshank as their noisy voices proclaimed.

It pleased me to rise early and go out looking for corncrakes in some of the most northerly fields in Britain. Theoretically, it was summer, but the grass had scarcely begun -to grow. The few corncrakes of Durness were skulkers in the nettle beds at the wall-sides. I saw one bird for almost five seconds.

On the day it was decided to make for Cape Wrath, we heard that the ferry across the Kyle of Durness was running for the first time in almost a week, and that the ferryman's wife—who had been shopping when the gale blew up—had been prevented from returning to husband and home across the water. She told me that rough water in the Kyle had kept them apart on the day they should have been celebrating their silver wedding.

Half a mile of sand and water lay between the landing and the cottage which appeared to be the only dwelling on the Cape Wrath peninsula. We watched the 'lazy' tide slowly over-run the sandbars and provide enough water for the small boat.

The first load consisted of 11 people, not forgetting a dog. While waiting for others to arrive, we looked over the Kyle on yet another scene in which northern Scotland vied for colour with the Caribbean. The sea ran against white beaches; the vegetation round about looked luxuriant in the bright light. Some of the sandbars held seals.

The road to Cape Wrath lay over peaty moorland with lochans. We heard that now and again, during naval exercises, shells are lobbed onto this dun-coloured landscape; a stray shell grazed a gate. (It has not opened smoothly since.) Faced with deciding whether to stand near the lighthouse on Cape Wrath or find another vantage point and actually see the Cape, we decided on the latter. As Fred said, 'I don't want a photograph with the camera pointing straight downwards!'

A peaty track we selected led us to a sandy bay. The northerly wind had whipped up the sea and the waves broke their backs on the beach in a flurry of foam and whirling sea birds. A great skua—the big brown buccaneer of the north Scotland seascape in the nesting season—would make a good living through harassing other birds returning with crops full of food.

We were invigorated by the view—by the turquoise and white of the ocean, culminating with the stack of Am Buachaille. Here was the Wrath, or 'turning point' of the old Norse seafarers. After battling westwards, they turned the dragonesque prows of their longboats southwards to the Hebrides. Far out to sea was the long, austere form of an oil tanker, a reminder of a daily threat of pollution along this wild and rocky coastline.

It was Ron who noticed the differences in the rocks of which this cliffscape was composed. Across the bay was the smooth grey gneiss, yet we stood on the Torridonian sandstone, tonally much warmer and a substance weathered to the stage where its many ledges had been colonised by plants and seabirds. The birds teemed around cliffs rising to 600 feet; the air was heady with the calling of the auks and kittiwakes. The many offshore stacks, remnants of the old coastline, should have had a reddish hue, being of sandstone, but they had been so plastered with the droppings of seabirds they resembled partly iced cakes.

To look over a 600-foot cliff was, as might be imagined, a dizzying sensation. Much was naked rock, but here and there plant life was profuse on great rockslips—diminutive Lost Worlds, where nature managed without human help.

One peaty slope was pock-marked by the entrances to puffin burrows. Puffins stood with grave expressions as, far below, the waves spent themselves against rock with dull thuds and the screaming of fretful kittiwakes, the nests of which had been plastered to the rock wherever there was a flange to provide a foundation.

Using my stomach as a sledge, I reached a point where I could almost touch a pair of razorbills. The calling of birds and the musty tang of droppings overwhelmed my senses, yet a few paces from the edge of the cliffs we walked over a tract of moorland where the only sound we heard was the whistle of the golden plover.

Next day the bonnet of our car was turned towards one of the many Scottish Tarbets, this being the boarding place for a short voyage to Handa, the 'sand island', where we saw once again the two main rocks in close association, the island of Torridonian sandstone outcropping near a foreland of Lewisian gneiss.

Our route from Durness to Tarbet lay across the 'ben and lochan' country. We were conveyed to Handa in a wee boat called the *Puffin*. The sea bed was either clean sand or thick weed, forming a striking and colourful pattern. Eastwards, the horizon was crowned by Sutherland's shapely hills. George reminded us that 'Sutherland', a name which to us signified far north, was the Norseman's 'south land'. He approached from the northern islands.

On a calm and sunny day, the white of the beach where Handa fronts the Sound was hurtful to the eyes. The sea was like crystal and the vegetation lush. I felt I could almost hear it growing as it responded to the warmth and light of the long northern days.

I viewed every detail of the sea bed as though through plate-glass. The waves quickly exhausted themselves on. the steep beach on to which the *Puffin* was driven; we were assisted from the boat and stepped onto a plastic beer bottle container—doubtlessly tossed here by the tide.

There followed a steady uphill walk, from east to west, on an island of 766 acres. The footpath began at sea level and ended abruptly at the edge of 400-foot cliffs. The hinterland was truly 'dreich'. A community of people had their clearings among tracts of peaty ground sporting heather; they raised potatoes which in due course were blighted; during the terrible potato famine of 1848, a famine which afflicted much of western Scotland and the islands, they were evacuated and went to America.

We knew the cliff edge was close when a fulmar petrel suddenly appeared before us, moving on stiffened wings, taking lift from a wind coming up beside the red cliffs from a spirited sea. Fred was fascinated by the 'engineless' fulmar. We peeped over the cliff edge and saw several birds on ledges; from them came a frog-like croaking.

Lower down were the ranks of the guillemots, packed on narrow ledges that must become very slippery from the guano, though when hard it may be one of the means by which the birds can keep their eggs from rolling off the ledge into the sea. The main ploy is the pear-shape of the guillemot egg, which causes it to revolve. Survival of the egg depends on it being covered by one of the parent birds at all times except for the moment when it is accepted from one by the other, for there is not a scrap of nesting material and the guillemot lives in a jostling world within an inch or two of a sheer drop into the sea.

Our packed lunch did not interest the sea birds. The herring gulls were too busy looking for other birds' eggs to trouble us unduly. What I remember about that lunch is that it included one of my pet hates—peanut butter. We followed a kilted photographer to the cliff edge where he set up a photographic tripod, fitted the camera to the top and prepared to take a photograph of the Great Stack, a vast remnant of the old shoreline. The Stack now rests on three legs, the sea having eroded much of the base away.

A small crowd of people watched the photographer rather

than the birds. Surely, the breeze would lift up the hem and the mystery of what the Scotsman wears under his kilt would be solved for us Sassenachs. The man stood in calm air near a turbulence that was threatening to turn fulmars inside out.

I recall the Torridonian red and the Lewisian grey; the green of the pastureland of Handa, where sheep and lambs were grazing, and the whitewashed rocks. I stared at the Great Stack's flat-dwellers—the rows of guillemots. Fred went skua-watching and soon located a great skua that seemed drawn to a tract of land near the main path. Fred was not encouraged to go looking for the nest but had a morbid interest in a creature that lives off the half-digested food teased from other birds.

We passed blow-holes, which sometimes are obscured by spray rising from water that has rushed into sea caves far below. We saw startled auks departing under water, using their wings as paddles; we marvelled at the silvery appearance caused by the air bubbles wreathing the plump bodies.

The height of the cliffs lessened as we walked eastwards; the afternoon sunlight had become brash, and the sea lay in streaks and patches of strong blues and unbelievable greens. The return to Tarbet was bumpy on a sea that responded to a freshening breeze. The boatman slackened off the engine power so that the little boat would not attempt to drive into the waves but would ride over them, which it did with a frill of sea-foam. While waiting for the boat to collect and return with others, we sat under a parasol in the garden of a cottage at Tarbet, drank strong tea and ate crab sandwiches. Fred listened to the *oo-ah-oo* of the eider drakes. I wandered off to stare with disbelief at the colour and clarity of this late afternoon near the top of Scotland. The greens and yellows of the iris were set against the inky-blue of a lochan, beyond which were the bare grey hills, like segments of a brain and a cloudless sky.

On Faraid Head north of Durness, we came across an astonishing puffinry, if the word can be used for a concourse of puffins at their nesting quarters. On the eastern side of the headland, where the ground fell away with a good covering of grasses but also with the ledge pattern that comes from a natural 'creep' of the surface, hundreds if not thousands of puffins were assembled, and others zoomed like podgy bees through the summer-warmed air.

We four assembled on the shore of Durness Bay to watch a sunset. It was 11.30 before the red orb of the sun reached the horizon and gave the bay its blood-red appearance; it was midnight when the sun slipped under the horizon. As we walked back to Durness, Ron said it might be worth looking about us for the sunrise!

13 THE LONGEST DAYS
Shetland

In the Shetland winter, the sun appears, spins for a wee while and is gone; in summer, any distinctions between day and night are blurred. Life goes on round the clock. Friends appear socially at 11 p.m. Someone has a bath at 2 a.m., and then decides to dress and go for a walk to post some letters.

In summer, there is no guarantee that the weather will be good. One day, a girl was seen helping with the peats in a bikini; on the following day she was sunbathing in dress and jumper! We drove to Aberdeen, had a meal and bought a newspaper. The weather forecast proclaimed: 'Sea moderate, with north-east swell tending to build.' It did.

One of the crew, noticing our anxious state, said: 'Och—there's been no wind for a fortnight; it must be like a millpond out there.' But the newspaper was correct and the *St Clair* rode on a moderate sea—a grey sea under a grey sky, with even the gulls looking mournful. Water glinted on the after-deck where rows of deck chairs were devoid of humanity; the canvas slapped itself in the salty wind.

Fred was amused by the bird-watchers. While they watched and logged the passing traffic—the guillemots and gannets, fulmars and shearwaters—he turned his binoculars on these earnest young men with their intense concentration on avian activity; human 'birds', it seemed, were ignored.

Watchman, what of the night? The weather conditions deteriorated, the bulkheads creaked a little, the engine pounded, the plumbing gurgled, and a view over the side was like looking at the dust-jacket illustration of *The Cruel Sea*.

I had my first coffee at 5.30 a.m. It was made at a machine of a blend of powders, mixed with hot water and taken in a cardboard cup. Some time during the night, the gulls had left us and the bonxies had moved in. We were overtaken by strings of guillemots, whose speed quickened as they became aware of the ominous forms of skuas. Two Arctic terns—the graceful sea swallows—had overwintered among the bergs of Antarctica and were now enjoying more of a life spent in almost continual sunshine.

Ron heard from a local man that the ship had recently removed a yard or two of pier at Lerwick during skeekit (fog). We also heard the improbable story of the skipper who set a course east from Lerwick in bad conditions having overlooked the isle of Bressay—on the shore of which the large craft came to a sudden grinding halt.

No misfortune befell us. The ship's crew was unfailingly helpful. The bows of the vessel were raised into a gigantic yawn; we drove onto Mainland, the largest island in the complex Shetland group...

We looked around at what remained when part of a continent, over a spell of millions of years, was eroded by rivers, pounded by the sea, pummelled by ice and subjected to a long period of rain, frost and wind. The process of erosion left something over 100 plots of land, scattered over a vast area like pieces in a tawny jig-saw.

To write thus is to give little indication of the character or appearance of these enchanted islands, for they are not composed of a single rock but of a number—red sandstone, limestone, schist and gneiss. Apart from the limestone, the rocks are non-porous, so that drainage is impeded; hence the peat and the heather and the brackish lochans. With relatively small plots of ground set in a sea which is frequently overswept by salt spray, few trees are seen on Shetland.

Fred was told by a local man about the special type of Shetland cabbage, the only type successful in this northern landscape. A proportion of the crop is allowed to grow to seed: it becomes tall and its yellow flowers rival the broom.

We drove northwards to Tofts Voe Pier, which was constructed as recently as 1951. The wind came to meet us, teasing the coarse moorland vegetation and ruffling the plumage of a greater black-backed gull. This bird straddled the corpse of an oystercatcher which had perished under the wheels of a speeding car.

The peat was being transported from moor to croft—not on ponyback, as had been the case for centuries, but in redundant plastic fertiliser bags of various colours, which were being lifted onto the backs of lorries. Old men told of the pony days, when half a dozen or so would form a string of animals, the peats stacked in baskets known as 'meshies'. It was that time of year when the ponies had foals at foot; these foals, running alongside, were initiated at an early age into the routine of moving peat. Hearing this, I recalled a Dales family who had a summertime 'flit' from one farm to another. They had but one horse and used it on a shuttle service. The foal of the year ran alongside.

We sailed to Yell. Spray swept over the bows of the ferry and left rime on the car windows. We were impressed by the buoyancy of an eider duck and her flotilla of black downy young; they moved in a turbulence of air and water. A bird photographer from Rochdale told us he would spend a fortnight on Yell photographing whimbrels—if the wind did not blow away his hides.

We, however, were merely passing through. Yell went by in a blur as we headed for the ferry to Unst. This craft bounced over the Sound to the wind's moaning and a tattoo of spray on the car roof. On my first visit to Unst, the Falklands Conflict was in progress and the television news had film of a landscape that was not dissimilar to Shetland.

The ferry passed one of the native boats, the inshore variety, said to be descended from the Viking longship. I was reminded of the Yorkshire coble, for which the same ancestry is claimed, though the Shetlander's craft is double-ended. We were later to see it drawn up on a beach—boat and harbour in one! The design has changed little through the centuries: one cannot improve on something that has 'fitness for purpose'.

Fred, Ron, George and I arrived on Unst, Britain's most northerly island. Unst! The name struck a note of finality. We had reached a point farther from the British mainland than St Kilda, where gaunt mountains leap out of the Atlantic. Unst was surely a name that came into use when the Norsefolk took over; and they were sparing with words. Ron, after scrutinising a map of the island remarked 'I feel at home here. The place is peppered with Norse placenames, just as in the Yorkshire Dales.' His study of the map produced 'fell' for hill, 'knowle' for hillock and 'setter', which he presumed was related to saeter, meaning the place of summer pasture.

Unst, a mere 47 square miles, lies farther north than Leningrad or Labrador; it has the Atlantic on one side and the North Sea on the other; its winter temperature is similar to Kew, and among its claims to fame is the unofficial British wind speed-record—177 m.p.h. Everything yields to the wind. We saw long, low ridges that were tenanted by diminutive ponies, sheep and lambs—small-scale creatures for a bleak environment.

The crofters' homes overlooked old-fashioned flower fields. Oystercatchers nested on the gravel beside the roads. A ringed plover led her family of chicks—wee creatures looking like bumble bees on long legs—in moist places where insect food abounded.

We played the 'most northerly' game, of course. At Haroldswick was the most northerly place of worship—not an ancient church sanctified by a Celtic saint, with an elaborately carved stone cross in a tussocky yard, but a Methodist chapel.

I once had the honour of preaching here—to a congregation composed of a few Methodists, a few members of the Church of Scotland, two Catholics and one Anglican.

Ron insisted on being taken to Skaw, the most northerly house in Britain. Before it came into view, we stopped to look over North Bay. The croaking of fulmars led to a search for birds, which we found in earthen 'pockets' on grassy slopes, staring unblinkingly across a shining sea.

Both great and Arctic skuas were nesting on the moor,—the Arctic skuas, long, sleek and nimble in the air, the great skuas diving like Stukas to within a few inches of our heads. A friend visiting Antarctica received a blow from a skua's webbed feet and was temporarily blinded. We were content to sit in the car and watch the birds. Two great skuas rested on a heather ridge some 40 yards away. Arctic skuas, dark phase birds, showed off their considerable power and grace in flight by harrying any sheep and lambs that ventured into their no-go area. Away across the moor, a light phase bird hovered just above the head of a grazing sheep until it moved away.

Skaw had an outbuilding made of a redundant boat, turned upside down and kept waterproof by regular applications of tar. Beneath the ancient timbers all manner of objects were being kept snuff-dry. Up to a dozen grey seals showed their faces in the sand-fringed bay.

We settled comfortably into an Unst routine which was not too demanding, except for the men working at the oil rigs some 80 miles offshore; they had to turn up on time to be taken to work by helicopter. For the rest of us, an hour or two did not matter. The crofter who had gone to bed late rose from that bed at 11 a.m. Returning home from a walk in the endless twilight at 12.15 a.m., we heard a hymn tune being played on what we took to be a Yamaha organ.

A crofter's wife, complete with hair-grips, told us that on the previous day, when the family was 'up at the peats', two pairs of whimbrel had been seen. I had long wanted to see what I think of as 'miniature curlew' on its nesting grounds. We settled in the lee of a dry ridge and watched two birds fly by with fast but shallow wingbeats, calling frequently—a rapid, even trilling.

We called at some petrol pumps to re-fuel the car and noticed that the pumps were rust-fringed, doubtless from the salt spray. Someone remarked that the shop at Baltasound used to have a notice: 'Ring once for bread, twice for milk and three times for petrol'. Fred emerged from another Shetland shop and claimed it had some items of clothing for sale that bore the wartime utility marks!

George, who had visited most of the outlying parts of Scotland, suggested a visit to Fetlar, which he did not know particularly well. To the rest of us, Fetlar meant snowy owls, birds at the southern rim of their great range; the owls on Fetlar had so often featured in magazines and on television.

It was a 20-minute voyage by ferry from Unst to Fetlar with much bird activity to see. Lines and chevrons of birds were returning from the fishing grounds, among them gannets and guillemots. They flew low, at an economic speed, until they became aware that predatory skuas had arrived. The gannets were soon taking evasive action and the guillemots seemed to increase the rate of their wingbeats until I had a feeling the wings would break off!

A great skua harried a gannet until it disgorged the fish from its crop, whereupon the skua collected an easily-won and already warm meal. Another skua simply flopped on a low-flying gannet, forcing it to the sea. Yet another luckless gannet was grasped by the tip of a wing and virtually shaken in mid-air.

Guillemots were flying close to the water. As the shadow of a skua came near them, some flopped onto the sea prepared to submerge.

Fred reported that a bird in flight ducked its head as a skua went by; A nearby puffin dived...

We found on Fetlar a softer, more fertile appearance than on the larger islands we had visited. Here, as elsewhere, we saw the remains of old settlements that had been thronged with people up to the time of the Clearances. We heard of the farming life on Fetlar at the edge of living memory, when in exceptionally hot spells, the families 'at the peats' rested up during the day and moved the turves back to their homes in the 'simmer dim'—a lingering twilight that impresses visitors from the south.

We saw our snowy owls. The helpful warden told us where to stand without causing a disturbance. The first of two owls rose from near the fifth fencing post, just as the warden had said! It was big and readily distinguishable from all other owls because of the gleaming white of its plumage. The appearance of the huge bird put the other nesters into a frenzy and the owl had little peace as it quartered the moor. Whimbrels went aloft and filled the air with their trilling.

I wanted to see a red-necked phalarope. Nae problem! We were directed to a roadside lochan, which is grandly named the Loch of Fenzie; it is used by phalaropes at feeding time. There was space for parking a car. While we waited, entertainment was provided by four red-throated divers! Arctic terns flew with creaky voices or bathed in the freshwater shallows. A fulmar sailplaned in an area out of sight of the sea.

The phalarope arrived without fuss. This dainty little bird, with a bill looking as fine as a needle and an orange patch at the back contrasting with its grey crown and white throat, spun in the shallows to bring up morsels of food, which it promptly collected with jabbing movements of that tiny bill. We marvelled at this wee creature which, like the white owl, is at the southern end of a vast breeding range—a range taking in tundra and northern forest areas—and which winters on the southern ocean.

The Fulmar had turned these northern islands into a huge nursery area. There must have been 100,000 fulmars on Fetlar alone. They were everywhere, from low coastal cliffs to the remains of old buildings. Fred knew that when he approached a structure like a 'plantie cro' it was ten-to-one there would be a fulmar nesting there. It proved to be the case on Fetlar when we found a line of these small drystone enclosures in which islanders gave crops like cabbages a good start in life, safe from the biting winds.. Fred took off his cap, put it on a stick and raised it above the wall. The response was a frenzied croaking sound. He peered over, and beheld a fulmar, crouching (doubtless on an egg) with lowered head and mandibles open.

The fulmar has a nasty trait: spitting' amber-coloured and evil-smelling oil at intruders. It does this with some accuracy up to three or four yards. Fulmar oil clogs the feathers of bird rivals, and the clothing of anyone spat upon will hold its pungent smell for ever. Fred was content to look and then to sneak quietly away.

Another day, we strode westwards to visit a family on a croft near a seal-haunted bay. It was also a walk back into history: we were entertained in the kitchen, where we sat beneath rows of dried fish suspended on lines and beside a stove that held the reek of peat. The crofter showed us his peat spade, with its redwood shank and feathered blade. Before any dry peat is brought into the house, it is knocked against the wall to dislodge any black beetles (which the crofter called 'hornclocks').

Ron asked for the name of the dry fish, and was told it was saithe, though in Shetland the species is called 'piltocks' and in other parts of Scotland has the unlovely name of 'colefish'. The Shetlanders catch saithe not far from land in summer; the fish are salted—'we like the salty taste as long as it is not too strong'—and are then hung to dry.

The method was explained to us. Fish are prepared two by two—the tails being tied together—and then slipped over an outside line for slow drying in the sunshine and breezes. The drying process is completed indoors. The saithe are then stored in boxes and eaten during the winter with potatoes.

Our evening meal featured another local delicacy— monkfish or 'mock scampi', purchased in Lerwick. Only the tail had been used, being cut into small pieces and cooked in breadcrumbs. In attendance on the monkfish were 'oven chips' from a shop with a frozen food department, as well as vegetables and salad. There followed some pineapple and cream (out of tins), plus oatcake and cottage cheese, both products of Shetland, the cheese having been made from the milk of goats.

Fred mentioned the diminutive sheep, which did not seem much bigger than Alsatian dogs. He was told that larger breeds—Cheviot and Suffolk—were kept on the low ground. 'We eat our own Shetland sheep from the hills; they are smaller and tastier than the others.' On this farm, three Shetland rams (or tups) mated with the ewes indiscriminately. Shetland sheep are 'of all colours—black, white brown, blue-grey'.

Fred, wandering off on Yell, returned with the news that he had met a farmer who was plucking, not clipping, a sheep. He had not imagined it. By an old sheep-fank, the farmer was rooing (plucking) a young ram. He hoped to sell the animal. He was using the old method so that the sheep would not look 'starved', as might be the case if it was shorn by machine.

It had indeed been a long way to Muckle Flugga. Now we planned our great expedition to Herma Ness, where the cliffs soar to a height of 657 feet and take the pounding of the restless Atlantic. We parked the car and trudged through an area of Unst where golfers use the knobbly hillocks as a course and the sheep are the unofficial green-keepers.

We were soon within sight of the radar scanner on Saxa Vord, where the cliff is almost 1,000 feet high. We passed close to the white-painted quarters erected for the families whose menfolk attend to the lighthouse on Muckle Flugga.

Fred enjoyed saying the name: Muckle Flugga! All along I had given the impression it was the most northerly point of Britain, but now I confessed that distinction belongs to the Outstack, a lump of smooth and naked rock which is fractionally farther north. 'Not even the gulls bother with it.' Equipped with thumb-sticks as a defence against the skuas we knew to be nesting on the moor, we followed an unmetalled track, beside a grassy bank where hundreds of orchids stood to attention and demanded to be noticed.

The domain of the skuas was undulating moorland with the sea on three sides. Both great and Arctic skuas were here. The former birds, the 'bonxies', circled with excited cries. Wherever we looked, there were bonxies. Ron mentioned that in a book he read it was stated that in 1920 only two pairs were to be found on Herma Ness (at the same time, one pair nested on Foula and now there are about 3,000 pairs on that westernmost island of the Shetland group).

There had been little rain for weeks; the path was snuff-dry, although boggy areas glowered with a lime green hue from the sphagnum moss. At this season of the year they were enlivened by the downy tufts of cotton grass (which is actually a sedge).

A pair of Arctic skuas harassed a sheep and its lambs, and in an area of small lochans, more than 100 great skuas—mainly non-breeders, we supposed—had gathered to wash and preen. The area round about the loch was paddled down through over-use. George recalled seeing kittiwakes washing the salt from their plumage at a freshwater lochan near the golf course.

A shower of rain developed from what had moments before been a clear sky; we sheltered in a bird-watchers' hut decorated within by entertaining cartoons featuring seabirds. The first time I saw them I took a photograph, which later I projected for the benefit of our local Women's Institute in Yorkshire. I had not read the graffiti, which were naughty in places. One of the least offensive comments was 'Sod the skuas'. As we looked from the hut on the slanting rain, a great skua assumed a favourite posture: neck jutting forward and upward, beak opened as it called, wings upwards and backwards—a quite dramatic pose.

The storm cleared. We completed the walk to the north coast in a stiff, cool breeze. Under our feet were peat and ling; above our heads flew the most northerly skylarks in Britain.

Into view came the long rock of Muckle Flugga, rising to some 200 feet where a 50-foot lighthouse had been set on the uptilted rocks. Muckle Flugga was not all grey: in places it was whitened by the recumbent forms of gannets and by the copious droppings.

George had heard that the lighthouse had been built by the Stevenson family of engineers. Ron, referring to the book, announced that it was the engineer David Stevenson who supervised the work in 1858 and that it cost £32,000. David was the uncle of Robert Louis Stevenson, who courageously visited Muckle Flugga. (He went from here to Speyside to write Treasure Island. Refer to the sketch map in that famous book and you will notice that the outline of *Treasure Island* is a little like that of Unst!)

Another storm arrived but the headland of Herma Ness appeared to cleave the storms. The most wearying job was donning and removing our waterproofs. In the end we did not bother to put them on. The rain seemed to pass on either side of us. We reached the edge of the sea and a dizzying cliffscape. Below us were jumbled rocks, grassy areas and a few sheer faces, populated mainly by puffins. A huge stack was white over with nesting gannets. The black-browed albatross, a species rarely seen north of the equator, turned up in this area for years and made for a specific ledge in a gannetry at The Point of Saito, here to make a nest and to wait for a mate which never arrived...

The features of the cliffs, just round the corner were imbued with frosty Nordic names—Clingera Stack, Bluescudda Kame, Orknagable and Valaberg among them. Our attention was held by the northernmost rocks—by the Outstack, known locally as Ootsta, and by Muckle Flugga.

On Outstack lived a mermaid who was beloved by two giants, Saxi and Herman, the dour guardians of Burra Firth. She managed to escape from them and swim northwards. The next landfall was the Arctic ice. In 1845, when Sir John Franklin went missing on his expedition to locate the North West Passage, his sorrowful widow was consoled by making a symbolic visit to the British rock nearest the Arctic. Despite its grim reputation as a friendless place, over-run by the ocean's swell, she was landed and prayed for the deliverance of her husband.

The first navigational light attached to Muckle Flugga appeared during the Crimean War when, a blockade of the White Sea having being instituted, the Navy requested an increase in the number of lights on Shetland. The most northerly light was never intended to be permanent, but local men found it invaluable and so it was replaced by Stevenson's tower. The workmen and their tackle were accommodated in an iron hut and the men used steps cut from the living rock to reach their precarious lodgings. Blocks of stone needed for the lighthouse were painstakingly raised on rail tracks laid on the steeply-angled rock. Work went on during a northern winter, when daylight lasted for just a few hours at a time.

Men became accustomed to the sound of waves breaking over the iron roof at their elevated lodgings. One breakfast-time a rogue wave shattered the door, flooded the hut and swept away many of their possessions.

The lighthouse keepers occupied a tower that remained watertight and surprisingly snug considering its exposed position. David Stephenson had a wall erected around the base to break the waves. The door of the lighthouse had a snug fit and weighed no less than a ton, yet once it was burst open by a gigantic wall of water.

Robert Louis Stevenson signed the visitors' book at the Flugga. It remained at the lighthouse until about 1930, when, fearing that some other visitor would steal the pages, the Northern Lights Commissioners in Edinburgh moved it to their headquarters for safety.

*   *   *

Fred, Ron, George and I stood on the north coast of Unst, on a speck of land some 138 nautical miles north of the Scottish mainland and 162 miles from the Norwegian coast. On a day of sunshine and shower, we three Yorkshiremen and a Scotsman allowed ourselves the luxury of a smile as we beheld the realisation of our dream—to come within sight of Muckle Flugga.

A fulmar glided past and gazed at us with its cold Arctic eyes...

INDEX

Index

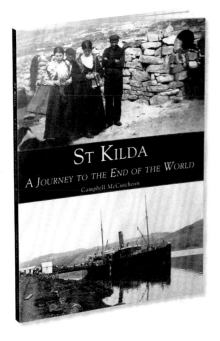

ST KILDA:
A Journey to the End of the World
Campbell McCutcheon

This is the story of a journey from Glasgow to St Kilda, using a unique photo album showing the tour that tourists would take when they went to visit the remote island group of St Kilda. Using a unique series of images, many taken on the island of Hirta, the route is traced through the Western Isles and takes in Coll, Tiree, Skye, North and South Uist and St Kilda itself. The album itself was found in a Bristol antiques fair and the author collected another 40 or so period images and brochures to trace the route from Glasgow's Anderston Quay down the Clyde to Village Bay in St Kilda.

235 x 165 mm | paperback | 128 pages | 120 illustrations

ISBN: 978 1 84868 057 9
PRICE: £12.99

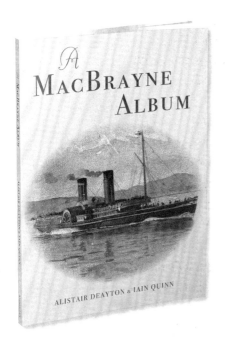

A MACBRAYNE ALBUM
Alistair Deayton & Iain Quinn

At the heart of this book is a unique collection of glass slides and glassmounted medium format negatives originally belonged to Captain Alex Rodger. Special attention is given to four steamers, *Columba*, the premier paddle steamer operating in UK waters, Iona, her predecessor on the Royal Route from Glasgow to Ardrishaig, and which had a remarkably long life of seventy-one years, and the two turbine steamers *Saint Columba*, which succeeded *Columba* on the Royal Route, and *King George V*, which made the Staffa and Iona cruise from Oban her own from 1936 to 1974.

235 x 165 mm | paperback | 160 pages | 128 black and white and 32 colour photographs

ISBN: 978 1 84868 428 7
PRICE: £14.99

NOW IN PAPERBACK

GLENCOE: THE INFAMOUS MASSACRE 1692
John Sadler

In the early hours of 13 February 1692, English Redcoats under the command of
Campbell of Glenlyon, who for the past week had been peacefully quartered on
the inhabitants of Glencoe, fell upon their MacDonald hosts. In the ensuing hours
38 defenceless men, women, and children were murdered in cold blood.

The massacre, sanctioned by the new king of England, William of Orange,
was initially covered up, but news of such treachery could not kept quiet and it
has become a cause célèbre of Scottish history. John Sadler reinvestigation of the
sources and contemporary accounts has yielded valuable new insights into why the
order was given, turning the previously excepted view of events on its head.

198 x 124 mm | paperback | 304 pages | 32 illustrations

ISBN: 978 1 84868 515 4
PRICE: £12.99

Available now from: www.amberleybooks.com